NEWPORT
SEVENTH DAY BAPTIST
TRILOGY

ENTERING INTO COVENANT
MEMBERSHIP RECORDS
MOTHER HUBBARD'S CUPBOARD

BY
ILOU M. AND DON A. SANFORD

Other Heritage Books by the author:

First Alfred Seventh Day Baptist Church Membership Records, Alfred NY

Membership Records of Seventh Day Baptists of Central NY State 1797-1940s

Membership Records of Seventh Day Baptist Churches in Western NY and Northwestern Pennsylvania 1800-1900

Published 1998 by

HERITAGE BOOKS, INC.
1540E Pointer Ridge Place
Bowie, Maryland 20716
1-800-398-7709
www.heritagebooks.com

ISBN 0-7884-0981-6

INTRODUCTION AND PURPOSE

The *Newport Seventh Day Baptist Trilogy* is designed for both the historian and the genealogist in response to the interest of those who have roots in the first Seventh Day Baptist Church in America founded in 1671 at Newport, Rhode Island.

Part One was written at the request of the Newport Historical Society as one of the goals of the Publishing Committee of the Society to publish a history of each of the four historic buildings owned by the Society:

(1) *The Wanton-Lyman-Hazard House*. The oldest existing house in Newport was built in 1675 by Stephen Mumford who was a member of a Seventh Day Baptist Church in England before migrating to America. It later belonged to the Ward family, prominent in Colonial America and members of Seventh Day Baptist churches in Rhode Island.

(2) *The Brick Market*: The city of Newport owns this1772 building which now houses a museum operated by the Newport Historical Society. It is a tribute to the industrial might of Newport in colonial days.

(3) *The Friends Meeting House*. Rhode Island was one of the first places where religious tolerance was granted to the Quakers. In 1699 the Quakers built what is considered the oldest meeting house still standing. It is a tribute to Rhode Island's commitment to religious tolerance which its neighboring colonies of New England did not grant.

(4) *The Seventh Day Baptist Meeting House*. The focal point of this 1730 edifice is the unique wine-glass pulpit pictured on the front cover. It was built and occupied by the Seventh Day Baptist Church until 1884 when it was sold to the Newport Historical Society for its meeting place and museum. The original manuscript of this history entitled: *Entering Into Covenant: The History of the Seventh Day Baptists in Newport* was abridged to meet specific needs and space limitations of the Newport Historical Society's *Quarterly Bulletin* (Vol. 66 Part I Summer 1994 No. 226). Permission was granted for this republication in its unabridged format.

Part II contains a compilation of the existing records of the membership of the church. The records of the church for its first twenty three years have been lost, but some information has been gleaned from copies of the journal of Samuel Hubbard, one of its founders, and some records from the First Baptist Church.

Part III of this trilogy derives its title from the Mother Goose nursery rhyme about Old Mother Hubbard who went to the cupboard to get her poor dog a bone and found it was bare. This could not have been written about a real Mother Hubbard named Tacy who lived in the seventeenth century. She and her husband, Samuel, were prime movers in the establishment of the Newport Seventh Day Baptist Church. Their three daughters brought into the "genealogical cupboard" the surnames of this extended family which have been repeated many times in the Seventh Day Baptist churches to the present time.

Pictured above is a Cramner translation of the New Testament and the Psalms now in the archives of the Seventh Day Baptist Archives. Of this Bible, Samuel Hubbard wrote in his journal, "Now I have a testament of my grandfather Cooke printed in 1549 which was hid in his bedstraw lest it be found and burnt in Queen Mary's days." Since the Bible came to the Society through Samuel's granddaughter, Naomi Burdick Rogers, it has sometimes been mistaken for the Roger's Bible belonging to the martyr John Rogers.

In 1995 this Bible was used by the author of this work in the dedication of his granddaughter, Tacy Camenga, the eleventh generation granddaughter of Tacy Hubbard who well have used it with her children and grandchildren 300 years ago.

TABLE OF CONTENTS

Part I

Part Two
Membership Records

5

Part III
Hubbard's Cupboard Is Not Bare

List of Abbreviations

CRR._____ SDB Historical So. accession number for
church records

abt	about
ad	admitted
b	born
bp	baptized
d	died
d/o	daughter of
m	married
s/o	son of
w/o	wife of

FOREWORD

Recollections Of A Visit
To The Old Meeting House

In 1934 Mrs. Maude Howe Elliott spoke at the Yearly Meeting of the New England Seventh Day Baptist Churches which was held in the old Seventh Day Baptist Meeting House in Newport. Mrs. Elliot was the daughter of Julia Ward Howe, the author of the popular <u>Battle Hymn of the Republic</u>, and the great grand daughter of Governor Samuel Ward. She recalled her experience as a small girl going with her mother to a service in that church some seventy years before.

"The past few moments have touched me deeply as I remembered associations with this beautiful old church. I will tell you about the church as I remembered seeing it the first time I entered it. My mother brought me here when I was a girl of about fourteen As we entered the church I was impressed by its great age. Everything was left as it had been after the last service. My mother found the Ward pew and we sat in it. On the altar was a plush cushion that evidently had been crimson but had faded to a lovely rose. On it was the Bible, which I hope is in the possession of the Historical Society, closed just as the minister had left it after the last service.

"The pews were as they had been when the church was in use and each pew had a name on it. From the time we entered the Ward pew my mother seemed to forget me. As we sat there I could not understand nor feel as my mother felt. It seems it must have been the way she felt when she wrote that beautiful hymn, *'In the beauty of the lilies, Christ was born across the sea, with a glory in his bosom that transfigures you and me. As he died to make men holy, let us die to make men free. While God goes marching on."*

Later Mrs. Elliot recalled an experience soon after the Russo-Japanese War of 1905. She had asked one of the Japanese generals how a small country like Japan could take up arms against a great country like Russia. "We went out and looked up to the sky, remembered our ancestors, and dared," he answered. Then Mrs. Elliot said,

"I have often thought of that and it has helped me. "When there has been some particularly trying situation, I have gone out and looked up to the sky and thought of my ancestors Richard Ward, the Colonial governor of the colonies, whose ancestors fought with Roger Williams for religious freedom and of that later one, his son, Samuel who was governor at the time of the Revolution. I do not remember when this church building was built but I know my ancestors worshipped in it; and it means much to me. Those are my recollections of it."[1]

Some of those same feelings can be shared with later generations who cross the threshold of the old meeting house. The old box pews are gone; the Bible on the altar has been removed, but the remembrance of ancestors, the Hubbards, the Burdicks, the Crandalls, the Langworthys, the Clarkes and the Maxsons are an inspiration to many in the present.

This picture of the box pews of the old Meeting House was printed from a glass negative of over a century ago. The box pews were generally rented to individual families, with one or two reserved for visitors. The seats in the balcony were occupied by servants or those who could not afford pew rent.

---

[1]Maude Howe Elliott, "Old Newport Church opens for Services --- Daughter of Julia Ward Howe Tells of Visiting Church in Youth" *The Westerly Sun October 21, 1934.*

Chapter 1

WHAT'S IN A NAME?

The registered name for the 1730 Meeting House owned by the Newport Historical Society is "The Seventh Day Baptist / Sabbatarian Meeting House." In its 1993 report the Preservation Cooperative, Ltd. recognized that according to the minutes of the Seventh Day Baptist Church from 1708-1817, the congregation referred to themselves and were referred to by others as Seventh Day Baptists, Sabbath Keepers, Sabbatarians, Sabbatarian Baptists and Church of Christ Observing the Seventh Day Sabbath. The name thus recognizes different titles for a single group of people who shared common beliefs and heritage. The Preservation Cooperative thus reported, "Clearly the establishment of a direct line from the present meeting house to the Seventh Day Baptists in America is indisputable."[2]

The names by which Seventh Day Baptists have been known signify three distinct beliefs and practices: (1) they were Baptists, (2) they held to the seventh day or Saturday Sabbath, and (3) they were Christians who accepted the validity of both Old and New Testament for their beliefs and practices.

1. Baptists: Their history is rooted in the Baptist branch of the Protestant Reformation which began in the early part of the seventeenth century. In England Baptists were first known as Separatists or Independents who rejected the state-church concept held by both Roman Catholics and the Church of England. Although many think of the Baptists in terms of the mode of baptism by immersion, the primary distinction in their early beginnings was the concept of believers' baptism. Like the Anabaptists of the sixteenth century European reformation, they rejected *paedo* or infant baptism which held that a person became a member of a church simply by being born into a Christian home or community. Baptists became a member of a covenanted community by personal profession of faith. With the Bible in the language and the hands of the people came the discovery that belief preceded baptism, The phrase, "Believe and be baptized," was the slogan of the Baptists. The practice of immersion or

---

[2] *The Seventh Day Baptist / Sabbatarian Meeting House 1729, Historic and Architectural Analysis Building Assessment,* for the Newport Historical Society Newport, Rhode Island 02840, Prepared by The Preservation Cooperative, Ltd. Newport, RI May 1993, p. 4.

"dipping" as it was often called came from Jesus' own baptism in the Jordan River and Paul's reference to baptism in Christ as being buried with him into death, and raised from the dead to walk in newness of life.[3]

Beginning about 1650 Seventh Day Baptists in England were a part of this Baptist movement. Many of them were active members of Baptist churches in England. Several served as pastors in Sunday churches, even after accepting the doctrine of the seventh day Sabbath. The first known Seventh Day Baptist in America was Stephen Mumford whose name, with that of his wife, appears on the role of the Tewksbury Baptist Church in England, a congregation which contained a number of Sabbath keepers. In time that group became the Natton Church in Gloucestershire which existed as a Seventh Day Baptist Church until the beginning of the twentieth century.

In the American Colonies, the first members of the Seventh Day Baptist Church were also Baptists who came to the Sabbath. The most prominent family in the Newport Seventh Day Baptist Church was the family of Samuel and Tacy Hubbard. Samuel came to Massachusetts from England in 1633 and Tacy came a year later. In 1647 they moved to Fairfield, Connecticut where they subscribed to Baptist ideas. Samuel gave his wife credit for taking the lead as he wrote in his journal:

> God having enlightened both, but mostly my wife, into his holy ordinance of baptizing only of visible believers, and being very zealous for it, she was mostly struck at and answered two times publickly; where I was also said to be as bad as she, and are threatened with imprisonment at Hartford jail, if not to renounce it or to remove; that scripture came into our minds, if they persecute you in one place flee to another: and so we did.[4]

In 1648 the family moved to Newport, Rhode Island where freedom of worship was granted much to the dismay of their Puritan neighbors in Massachusetts. Such was the degree of tolerance in Rhode Island that the noted Puritan preacher, Cotton Mathers, called Rhode Island "a cesspool" of religious practice. In his *Ecclesiastical History of New England,* Mather wrote that "there never was held such a variety of religions together on so small a spot of ground as in Rhode Island: Antinomians, Familists, Anabaptists, Anti-sabbatarians, Arminians, Socinians, Quakers, Ranters --

---

[3] Romans 6:3-4.

[4] Samuel Hubbard, *Register of Mr. Samuel Hubbard* (transcript of excerpts with notes by Isaac Backus, ca 1775) B 136 i. Mss, Rhode Island Historical Society Library, Providence, (microfilm copy MF 1989.4 SDB Hist. Soc. Lib.) 4-5 (10 May 1647).

everything in the world but Roman Catholics and real Christians."[5] The fear which the Puritans held for the Baptists was real, for it threatened their whole political as well as social and religious community. In a government where political citizenship was dependent upon membership in a state church, waiting for profession of faith eliminated a large segment of the population from citizenship.

2. Seventh Day Sabbath Observance: The name Seventh Day Baptist / Sabbatarian Meeting House recognized that the members held to the practice of observing the seventh day of the week, Saturday, rather than Sunday which was held by the majority of Christians. William Brackney in his book: *The Baptists,* gave an overview of Baptist history in England. After describing the emergence of the General and the Particular Baptists in terms of their concept of salvation, he noted the origins of the Seventh Day Baptists as a part of the separatist movement.

> A third stream of the Baptist persuasion also demands
> attention. Smaller in numbers, more heavily persecuted, and no
> less adamant about their faith were the Seventh Day Baptists.
> In the biblicism of the age when the Scriptures were being
> constantly reexamined as a standard of Free Church doctrine
> and practice, it is not surprising that a person or church should
> conclude that keeping the Sabbath was an inescapable
> requirement of biblical Christianity.[6]

The term *Sabbatarian* was probably used as a derogatory reference in the beginning much the same as the term *Christian* may have been used of those in the Antioch Church as reported in Acts 11:26. But it became a mark of distinction among the Seventh Day Baptists even though the term *Sabbath* from which it was derived was used by the Puritans in regard to Sunday. Many of the records of the Newport Church did use the term Sabbatarian. The tomb stone of Governor Thomas Ward documents that "He was a member of the Sabbatarian Church of this Town and Attended to Doctrines of his Saviour". The first history of the Seventh Day Baptists printed in 1811 by Henry Clarke was entitled, *A History of the Sabbatarians or Seventh Day Baptists in America containing their Rise and Progress to the year 1811, with their Leaders' Names and their*

---

[5] Cotton Mather, *Magnalia Christi American; or The Ecclesiastical History of New England* (New York, reprint 1967), II, 520-521. Cited by Edwin Gaustad, *Baptist Piety, The Last Will and Testimony of Obadiah Holmes* (Grand Rapids, MI: Eerdmans Publishing Co. 1978) 21.

[6] William H. Brackney, *The Baptists,* (New York: Greenwood Press, 1988) 6-7.

Distinguishing Tenets.[7] It was not until 1817 that their General Conference officially adopted the name Seventh Day Baptist.[8]

In legal matters, however, the name Seventh Day Baptist was generally used. According to the deed records, Arnold Collins sold to Joseph Bennett a house and land for the Seventh Day Baptists near the corner of Spring and Barney Streets, "called and known by ye name of ye Seventh Day Baptist Meeting House.."[9] The church minutes for April 29, 1718 empowered execution of a deed of sale "in order that the church or congregation of Seventh Day Baptists may have full and lawful authority to claim challenge and demands all rights or profits arising. for any other use than the true intent of the land was bought and purchased for."[10]

3. Christians Observing the Laws of God and Faith of Christ: Both in England and in parts of America during the seventeenth and eighteenth centuries the keeping of the biblical Sabbath was often interpreted as being Jewish. Thus in 1705 when a sister church was founded in Piscataway, New Jersey they chose a name which clearly distinguished it as Christian: *The Church of Christ Keeping the Commandments of God and the Faith of Jesus Christ living in Piscataway and Hopewell in the Province of New Jersey.*[11] This name reflected both their Christian allegiance and their obedience to the Ten Commandments. However, as their relationships with the churches of like faith in New England increased, they adopted the name Seventh Day Baptist and in 1878 "to comply with the state laws it is legally known as the Seventh Day Baptist Church of Piscataway, New Jersey."[12]

Thus the name: Seventh Day Baptist / Sabbatarian Meeting House gives recognition to different names which were used by Seventh Day Baptists in a continuous history covering over three centuries beginning in England, continuing in Rhode Island, spreading across the nation and into mssions around the world. It is documented by deeds, by church records and by family names

---

[7] Henry Clarke, *A History of the Sabbatarians or Seventh Day Baptists.....* (Utica, NY: by the author 1811) title page.

[8] Conference Minutes, *SDB Year Book* (1817), 5

[9] Land Evidence Records, Vol. 1, p. 39 Newport Historical Society Collection.

[10] Church Minutes document 1400 Newport Historical Society Library dated 29 of 4 mo. 1718 pg. 24.

[11] Minutes of the *SDB* Church of Pisacataway, Aug.19, 1705.

[12] Record of such action may be found in the middlesex County Clerk's office on page 15 Book B -- Incorporated Societies.

Chapter 2

THE FOUNDING OF A CHURCH:
ITS PEOPLE

Seventh Day Baptists are a covenant people based on a concept of regenerate membership, believers' baptism, congregational polity, and scriptural basis for beliefs and practices. The history of the Newport Seventh Day Baptist is a history of people and their struggle to maintain their covenant relationships while being true to what they perceived to be the scriptural basis for beliefs and practices, particularly as it involved their belief in the Sabbath. Thus no one person can be considered the founder of the church with authority over others.

The original records of the founding of the church have been lost, however much of the history has been preserved by Samuel Hubbard and later by Baptist historians, Isaac Backus and John Comer. The Comer document of ca. 1728 records the covenant of the church as follows:

> After serious consideration and seeking God's face among our Selves for the Lord to direct us in a right way for us, and our children so as might be for God's glory and our Souls good and others Example, We Entered into Covenant with ye Lord and with one another and gave up our Selves to God and one another to walk togather in all God's Holy Commandments and Holy Ordinances according to what the Lord had Discovered to us or Should Discover to be his mind for us to be obedient unto; with Sence upon our Hearts of great need to be watchfull over one another, Do promise So to do, and in Edyfying and building up one another in our Most holy faith-----

This 7th Day of December 1671. Viz.

Males: William Hiscox   Females: Tacy Hubbard
          Samuel Hubbard   Rachel Langworthy
          Steven Mumford   _____ Mumford.
          Roger Baster[13]

---

[13] John Comer, *History of Baptists in Newport* from Franklin Trask Library, Andover-Newton Theological School, Isaac Backus Papers c.s. MSS 1984-1 Box 6 pages 1-2.

The Backus document is basically the same with minor variation in wording, but dates the covenant December the 23rd 1671. It also lists Stephen Mumford's wife as Mary rather than Ann as found on her tombstone and in other records. There was a Mary who was the wife of Stephen Mumford, Jr. Furthermore, the Backus account follows the covenant with the notation:

> ....five of ye above mentioned were members of ye Church and Stephen Mumford and his wife were never joined because of non observance of ye 7th Day for they were members of a 7th Day Church in England --- then the 3rd Church was Constituted and Mr. William Hiscox was chosen Pastor. His Successors in ye Ministry were Mr. William Gibson and Mr. Joseph Crandall. About ye year 1705 they erected a Meeting House for Sabbath worship.[14]

Who were these people who gave rise to this third Baptist Church in Newport?

Stephen Mumford: The first known Seventh Day Baptist in America was Stephen Mumford who arrived in New England about 1664. Correspondence between the Sabbathkeepers in Rhode Island and the Bell Lane church in London led some to conclude that he was a member of that church. However, more recently discovered documentation places him in the Tewksbury Baptist Church in Gloucestershire, about one hundred miles west of London. The list of Sabbath keeping members of that church included the pastor, John Cowell; John Purser who became a long time leader of the Seventh Day Baptist congregation in Natton near Tewksbury; and Stephen and Ann Mumford.[15] Samuel Hubbard confirms this relationship as he wrote, "By a leter from John Cowell to Mr. Mumford dated Tewksbury 14th 7m, 1671, it appears that Mumford was originally of that place."[16]

Stephen Mumford left England shortly after a period of anti-Sabbatarian sentiment had disrupted the Tewkesbury church. It was also in a period of growing intolerance against Baptists in general by the restored monarchy under Charles II. It is possible that these conditions influenced the Mumfords' decision to come to Rhode Island where religious freedom

---

[14] *The Backus Papers*, Vol. 2, page 21 in Rhode Island Historical Library (copies in MS 1989.30 Seventh Day Baptist Historical Library, Janesville, WI.)

[15] Tewksbury Baptist Church record book, leaves 21v-22r, researched by Oscar Burdick.

[16] *Samuel Hubbard's Journal*, RI. Historical Records Survey WPA Providence, RI 1940. p. 64.

was granted. There appears little documentation to support the theory that Stephen Mumford was sent as a missionary to Rhode Island by the churches in England. There is no record of his having preached or administered the sacraments in the church. The names of his children do not appear on any of the church rolls. It is often presumed that it was largely through his infuence that the other Sabbatarians in New England came to the Sabbath. Yet the Sabbath was not a new concept among Christians in New England in the middle of the seventeenth century. There was a great deal of communication between England and its colonies; and many books and tracts were circulated from England.

The decade of the 1650s was a period when the Sabbath was debated in many circles in England. As early as 1628 Theophilus Brabourne, a priest in the Church of England published, *A Discourse upon the Sabbath Day* in which he attempted to persuade the Church of England to accept the validity of the seventh day Sabbath. In 1650 a Baptist, James Ockford, published a book entitled, *The Doctrine of the Fourth Commandment, Deformed by Popery, Reformed and Restored to its Primitive Purity*. Its publication so undermined the observance of the "Lord's Day" that Parliament ordered all copies to be burned and the author punished. In 1659 a debate concerning the Sabbath was held in the Stone Chapel beside St. Paul's Cathedral in London which drew hundreds of people. The works of Edward Stennett, and the organization of a church by Francis Bampfield while in prison took place prior to the acceptance of the Sabbath by the nucleus in Newport. These events could hardly have escaped the attention of people on both sides of the Atlantic.[17] Furthermore it was the study of the Bible in England which brought the people to the Sabbath, and most certainly played a major role, along with the witness of immigrant witnesses such as the Mumfords, in the acceptance of the Sabbath doctrine in the American colonies.

Legal records show that Mumford owned property on which he built a home which has been described as "one of the finest examples of early colonial architecture in New England." This house, the Wanton-Lyman-Hazard House, located at 17 Broadway is the oldest remaining house in Newport. It has been restored and is in the possession of the Newport Historical Society. The records show that on his death in 1701 the property was left to his son Stephen, Jr. who was a merchant. The house later was sold to Richard Ward, a member of the same church as that of

---

[17] cf. Don A. Sanford, *A Choosing People, the History of Seventh Day Baptists* (Nashville, TN: Broadman Press for the SDB Historical Society, Janesville , WI 1992) ch. 4.

Mumford.[18] The ownership of such a house, and Mumford's ability to make a return trip to England suggests that he also may have been a merchant. Few ministers of that day had resources for such expenditures. Rhode Island Land Evidence Records note that Stephen Mumford entered into land purchases with Robert Ayres who later bought a huge tract of land in Southern New Jersey where the Shiloh Seventh Day Baptist church was formed in 1737. Katherine Ayers, wife of a Robert Ayres, is buried in the Mumford plot in Newport suggesting some family connections.

Another discrepancy in some of the early accounts concerns Mumford's supposed membership in the First Baptist Church of Newport, often referred to as Dr. John Clarke's Church, now the United Baptist Church. The microfilm listing of the membership roll of that church lists Stephen Mumford as being a member, but does not list his wife. A closer examination of the oldest copy of the membership list reveals that Stephen Mumford's name may have been inserted by a different hand, between no. 53, Roger Baster who joined in 1663 , and no. 54, Richard Dingley, the third pastor of the church who joined in 1690. This appears to be confirmed by the Backus account mentioned above and the detailed account of the separation of the Sabbath keepers found in the First Baptist Church records describing the separation which took place in 1671. The account begins:

A brief and faithful Relation of the Difference between those of this church and those who withdrew their communion from it with ye Causes and Reasons for the Same -- the Brethren and Sisters were:

William Hiscox	Tacey Hubbard
Roger Baster	Rachel Langworthy
Samuel Hubbard	

Each of whome left ye Church on ye 7th day of December 1671.[19]

Later the account states, "After many things of this nature and being weary of ye contest those five Sabitarians meet together to consider what they may safely do.... after seeking ye Lord they 5 concluded to withdraw since there was no hopes of peace in ye church while they remained."[20]

---

[18] Ronald Potvin, "The Architectural History of the Wanton-Lyman Hazard House" in *Newport History, Bulletin of the Newport Historical Society,* Vol. . 62, Part 2 , Spring 1989, Number 214, p. 47.

[19] Typescript Excerpts from Newport First Baptist Church Book Describing Differences with Seventh Day Baptists in 1671. MF 1987.1 in Seventh Day Baptist Historical Society p. 1.

[20] *ibid.* p. 8.

Nonetheless, in spite of some of the traditions which have grown up around Stephen Mumford, he was important as being the first Seventh Day Baptist of record in America. As a layman in the church, he shared his convictions with others. It is clear also that Stephen Mumford provided a link with the Sabbath keepers in England and on a return trip to England in 1675, he brought back Elder William Gibson who served as the second pastor of the Newport Seventh Day Baptist Church.

Samuel and Tacy Hubbard: Stephen Mumford may have been the first Seventh Day Baptist in America chronologically, but the Hubbards were the most influential in establishing the first Sabbath keeping Christian church on this side of the Atlantic. Their importance lies not only in what they did and said, but also in the record that they provide for the history of the period in which they lived. Much of Samuel Hubbard's journal and correspondence was copied and extracts have been used by historians as a primary source for the thoughts and actions of the last half of the seventeenth century.

Samuel Hubbard was born in Mendelsham, England in 1610 and emigrated to Salem, Massachusetts in 1633. The following year he moved to Watertown and joined the church in 1635 "by giving account of my faith." Tacy Cooper came to Dorchester in 1634 and joined the church there. Samuel and Tacy were married in 1636 at Windsor, Connecticut. The Hubbards made several moves during the next few years. At Springfield they were instrumental in gathering a church. In 1647 they moved to Fairfield, where they subscribed to Baptist ideas.[21] It was here that both Samuel and Tacy came into sharp conflict with the authorities who threatened them with imprisonment because of their Baptists convictions. To escape persecution, they moved to Newport, Rhode Island where they were baptized by John Clarke in 1648 and joined the Baptist Church. In a letter written in 1668 to his cousin, John Smith of London, Hubbard described his condition:

> Thro' God's great mercy the Lord have given me in this wilderness a good, diligent, careful, painful & very loving wife; we thro' mercy live comfortably, praised be God, as coheirs together of one mind in the Lord, traveling thro' this wilderness in our heavenly Sion, knowing we are pilgrims as our fathers were; & good portion being content therewith. A good house as with us judged, & 25 acres of ground fenced in, & 4 cows which give milk, one young heifer and 3 calves,

---

[21] Ray Greene Huling, "Samuel Hubbard of Newport: 1610 - 1689" (n.p.: n.d.) Reprinted from *Narraganset Historical Register* 5 (Dec. 1887): 1-15.

& a very good mare; a trade, a carpenter, & health to follow,
& my wife very diligent and painful; praised be God.[22]

His property was in what was later named Middletown near that of Obadiah Holmes and John Clarke, leaders in the First Baptist Church. From an article in the *Literary Diary of Ezra Stiles, President of Yale University,* there is a copy of an old memorial stone[23] which reads:

Ebenezer
Samuel Hubbard aged 10 of May 78 yeres
Ould Tase Hubbard aged 27 Sep. 79 yeres and 7 mons
4 Jen. maryed 51 yeres 1688
14V psal 4. God have given us 7 children 4 ded 3 living
Ruth Burdick 11, 1 ded 10 living
Rachel Langworthy had 10 children 3 ded 7 living
Bethiah Clark 9 living.
Great Grandchildren
Naomi [B] Rogers 1 ded 4 alyfe
Ruth [B] Philips 1 ded 4 alyfe
Judah [C] Maxson
Thomas Burd

A further note from the Stiles Diary explains: "I took this inscription off a gravestone in a family burying place on Baptist Berkeley's White Hall farm on Rd Isld, about A. D. 1763. Collector Robinson bought the lease about 1765 and demolished the gravestones and put them into a wall: so all is lost." He interpreted this to mean that the stone was erected on September 27, 1688 when Samuel was 79 years old on May 10, Tacy was 79 years and 9 months old and that they had been married for 51 years on January 4 of that year. The Psalm reference was Psalm 145:4 which reads, "One generation shall praise thy works to another." The superscript letters with Naomi, Ruth and Judah shows lineal decent from Burdick and Clark.[24]

---

[22] Hubbard *Journal* p. 38.

[23] The term *Ebenezer* means a memorial stone set up to commemeorate divine assistance such as that found in 1 Samuel 7:12 when Samuel took a stone and set it up after a victory over the Philistines, saying "Hitherto the Lord has helped us."

[24] Ezre Stiles, *Literary Diary of Ezra Stiles, Pres. of Yale University,* Vol. III pg. 82, cited in *The Langworthy Family* compiled by WIlliam F. Langworthy, (Rutland VT: Tuttle Publishing Co: 1940) p. 5-6.

About 1987 a stone bearing the name Samuel Hubbard was found in a flower bed next to Whitehall on Berkeley Avenue in Middletown and in 1993 was in the basement of Middletown Historical Society's Paradise School Museum. The date is so obliterated that it is difficult to make positive identification with the father or either of his two sons bearing that name. The stone wall which still borders White Hall causes one to wonder if other similar stones lie hidden within the wall.

Almost from the beginning, Samuel was recognized as a leader within the church. When John Clarke, Obadiah Holmes and John Crandall were arrested and imprisoned in 1651 while visiting a Baptist brother in Lynn Massachusetts, Samuel Hubbard was one of those who was sent by the church to visit them in prison and attempt to secure their release.[25] In 1657 Hubbard accompanied Obadiah Holmes on a missionary tour to some of the Dutch settlements on Long Island, at Gravesend, Jamaica, Flushing and Hampstad.[26]

Although Samuel Hubbard was a recognized leader in the Baptist Church, Tacy appears to have been the dominant force in the Seventh Day Baptist Church. As mentioned previously, Tacy was the first to have been "enlightened into [God's] holy ordinance of baptizing only of visible believers."[27] Nearly twenty years later, Samuel Hubbard entered into his Journal the note:

> My wife took up keeping the lord's holy 7th day
> Sabbath the 10 day March 1665. I took it up 1 day April
> 1665. Our daughter, Ruth 25 Oct. 1666. -- Rachel-- Jan.
> 15 1666--Bethiah -- February 1666. Our son Joseph
> Clarke 23 Feb. 1666.[28]

Her role is also noted by Edwin Gaustad's account of the debate which led to the 1671 separation of the five from the church of John Clarke. "Joseph Torrey thought that the congregation ought to hear from someone besides Hiscox, and after much discussion Tacey Hubbard was allowed to summarize the reasons for their not taking communion with the rest of the church."[29]

---

[25] cf. Edwin Scott Gaustad, *Baptist Piety: The Last Will and Testimony of Obadiah Holmes,* (Grand Rapids, MI: Christian University Press and Eerdman's Publishing Co., 1978) 52.

[26] Hubbard, *Journal* p. 9

[27] Hubbard, *Journal* p. 4-5.

[28] Hubbard, Journal p. 9-10. Note: The old style calendar was used in which the new year began in March rather than January.

[29] Gaustad, Baptist Piety p.56. Hubbard records this incident, writing: "Then Br. Hiscox began but they would not let him --every one

In a letter to John Thornton of Providence in December 1686, Hubbard summed up their religious pilgrimage with the words:

My wife and I counted this year 1686: My wife a creature 78 years, a convert 62 years, married 50 years, an independent & joined to a church 52 years, a baptist 38 years, a sabbath keeper 21 years. I a creature 76 years, a convert 60 years, an independent & joined to a church 52 years, a baptist 38 years and a sabbath keeper 21 years. We are by rich grace born up & adorned with rich mercies above many, as to have all three daughters in the same faith & order & 2 of their husbands, and 2 of my grand daughters and their husbands also with us.[30]

The Hubbards had seven children, but only three daughters lived to full maturity. Naomi was born in 1637 and died ten days later. About a year later a second daughter, also named Naomi, died at age six; Ruth was born in 1640 and married Robert Burdick; Rachel, born in 1642, married Andrew Langworthy; Samuel, was born in 1644, but died soon after birth; Bethiah, born in 1646, married Joseph Clarke. Another son, also named Samuel, was born in 1649, but died at age twenty with no children.[31] The Hubbard name was carried on by a brother and other members of the larger family, but the religious heritage of Samuel and Tacy was multiplied many fold in their daughters, sons-in-law, and grandchildren for generations. Ruth Hubbard married Robert Burdick, and the Burdick name is prominent in many Seventh Day Baptist churches to this day. Through Robert and Ruth Burdick's daughters: Naomi, Ruth, Deborah, and Tacy, the names of Rogers, Phillips, Crandall, and Maxson are found in later generations of church families. One generation further removed, the children of Rev. Joseph and Deborah (Hubbard) Crandall brought in such names as Wells, Stillman, Saunders, Lewis, and Babcock,

Similarly, the Hubbard's third daughter, Bethiah married Joseph Clarke, the nephew of Dr. John Clarke, the founder of the First Baptist Church in Newport. Her husband was mentioned by Hubbard as "son, Clarke," who came to the Sabbath with others in the family in 1666. Their daughter, Judith, married John Maxson Jr. who became the third pastor of the Westerly Church. Another daughter, Bethiah, married Thomas Hiscox, the fourth pastor of that same church. Two other daughters, Mary and

---

must answer for himself lest others be led by him: so they named me, but I would not be first: then my wife laid down three grounds...."

[30] Hubbard *Journal* p 146-147.
[31] Hubbard *Journal* p. 7 & 30.

Susanna, were progenitors of some of the Champlins and Babcocks within the denominational line.[32]

Although both Ruth and Bethiah shared the convictions of their parents their distance from Newport kept them from direct involvement in the separation from the Baptist church in Newport. They were listed as members of the Baptist Church, Ruth having joined in 1652 along with her future husband, Robert Burdick, with Bethiah joining in 1661. By 1671 they were settled in the western portions of Rhode Island where their families were instrumental in the establishment of a branch of the Seventh Day Baptist Church at Hopkinton, then called Westerly. In a 1669 letter signed by Ruth Burdick and Joseph Clarke of Westerly written to Thomas Olney of Providence, there is an affirmation of their "practice of keeping his holy sabbath, even the 7th day."[33] In turn, Samuel Hubbard in June 1660, wrote a response to some of their concerns emphasizing the scriptural basis for their position, revealing how support was shared with the whole family. Both Ruth and Bethiah, along with their husbands and many of their children, were listed in the 1692 membership roll of the Newport Seventh Day Baptist Church.

Rachel Langworthy: Rachel, the other daughter of Samuel and Tacy Hubbard, remained in Newport and thus was one of the charter members of the Newport Seventh Day Baptist Church. At the time she was married to Andrew Langworthy, an active member of the First Baptist Church since 1652. According to Hubbard's Journal, Andrew "joined to our church today Feb. 1676."[34] Their son, John, and his wife, Elizabeth, appear on the list of members in 1692. Although their son, Samuel, does not appear on any of the church rolls, his daughter, Ann, married the son of Rev. Joseph and Deborah (Burdick) Crandall. It is through this union of Joseph Crandall, Jr. and Ann Langworthy that a major branch of the Crandall line continued within the Seventh Day Baptist churches. From the records, it appears that it was often the women who brought their husbands and children into the church, a pattern which began with Tacy and has continued with considerable frequency among Seventh Day Baptist families to this day.

William Hiscox: The pastor of the group which formed the Seventh Day Baptist Church was William Hiscox. He was born in 1638, thus was twenty-eight years younger than Samuel Hubbard. He became the spokesman for the Sabbatarians in their dispute with the First Baptist

---

[32] For a more complete summary see Part II of this book.

[33] Hubbard, *Journal* p. 44-45.

[34] Hubbard, *Journal* p. 11

church of which he had been a respected member. He accepted the Sabbath in 1666, about the same time as the Hubbards embraced it, and continued in full fellowship with the Baptist Church until the separation in 1671. Evidence of his ability and position in that church is his involvement in the trial of Thomas Goold (sometimes spelled Gould), the recognized founder of the Baptist church in Boston.

Beginning in 1655 Thomas Goold of Cambridge, Massachusetts became convinced of the error of infant baptism and carried on a running battle with the established church. In 1665, he and eight others signed a covenant organizing themselves into a Baptist church, or as they described it "a church of Christ on antipedobaptist principles." After numerous imprisonments and court appearances, the Governor and General Council ordered a "full and free debate" in 1668 hoping that such a trial would put the issue to rest. Six ministers from the established Puritan churches were chosen to refute once and for all the Baptist position. In defense, Goold and five others from his congregation were chosen. Because of the significance of this debate to the religious community of all the colonies, the Newport church of John Clarke appointed four members in support of their Baptist brethren. Two of those four were drawn from the Sabbatarian members, William Hiscox, and Samuel Hubbard. A third was John Crandall who had moved to the mainland at Westerly (Hopkinton) where he pastored the Baptist Church. He later accepted the Sabbatarian position and became the pastor of the Westerly branch of the Seventh Day Baptist church.(His son, John Jr., married Hubbard's granddaughter, Deborah Burdick.) The fourth representative of the Newport Church was Joseph Torrey who was to play a major role as a spokesman for the anti-sabbatarian position in the controversy with the Seventh Day Baptists.

This debate may have had considerable influence on William Hiscox and the church at Newport, for as William G. McLaughlin wrote, "The Baptists had no real spokesman and no unified or consistent line of argument." Three points were argued by the Baptists. The first point was the Non-Separatist Baptist position which held that while the issue of baptism and polity were important, they were not sufficient grounds for separation; they still could have communion and worship with those who disagreed. The second position called for the right of a different form of Puritanism existing as a parallel denomination with its own churches but still within the existing framework of the Puritan system. They still considered the Puritan church to be the true church even thought they were in error on the point of infant baptism. The third position was one of complete separation. Proponents of this position held that "the Puritan churches were so corrupt as to be null and void, if not antichristian, and that only the Baptist position was true to the gospel."[35] In a sense these positions reflected the thinking of the Puritans, the Separatists and the Independents in the English Reformation of the preceding century. As participants in the proceedings in Boston, William Hiscox and Samuel Hubbard could hardly have escaped the significance of the issues in relation to their own differences with the Baptists.

Roger Baster: Little is known of Roger Baster whose name appears with the other charter members of the Sabbatarian Church. His tombstone in the Newport Common Burial Ground identifies him as a bachelor, and a blockmaker, who died 23 Apr. 1687 at age of 66 yr, making his calculated year of birth as 1621. His occupation as a blockmaker connected him with the shipyard, where blocks, or pulleys were much needed by sailing ships. The stone also identifies him as one of the founders of a church observing the 7th Day Sabbath of the Lord in New England, with the date of December 23, 1671. Hosea Clarke who copied the inscription in 1848, called this the most ancient record of Seventh Day Baptists in America, "engaven on stones."[36]   Samuel Hubbard recorded a letter dated 1667 from a prisoner on Plymouth Island addressed to Roger Baster, listing the names of several people who "went over to your parts since you did," some of whom were formerly members of the church at Dartmouth.[37] This may indicate that he was a more recent immigrant from England than the others. However he came to the Sabbath conviction in 1666 about the same time as the Hubbards. In other references, Roger Baster appeared in a supporting role lending his signature to letters from the church, or as in the debate with the Baptist Church, saying, "Brother Hiscox hath spoke my mind."[38]

Roger Baster had no children to carry on the family name, or be revered by the genealogists. He took no leadership role for which he is remembered, yet he represents a host of people who remained firm in their convictions and gave support to others. Without such people, the role of the leaders would be fruitless.

---

[35] William G. McLaughlin, *New England Dissent 163-1833, The Baptists and the Separation of Church and State* (Cambridge, MA: Harvard University Press 1971) Vol I p. 62-63. Information from the Thomas Danforth Papers in Massachusetts Historical Society's *Proceedings,* LXXVI (1964) 91-133.

[36] *The Sabbath Recorder*, vol 5:17 October 13, 1848 p. 66

[37] Hubbard, *Journal* p. 42.

[38] Hubbard, *Journal* p. 65.

Chapter 3

THE FOUNDING OF A CHURCH:
A CRITICAL DECISION

The date December 23, 1671[39] is generally given as the birthdate for the first Seventh Day Baptist church in America; yet there was considerable time of gestation accompanied by discomfort and labor pains. Edwin Gaustad, in his biographical sketch of Obadiah Holmes, one of the key figures in the discussions which led to the separation, pointed out that the six years between Tacy Hubbard's first acceptance of her Christian duty to the separation in 1671, "were years of painful decision and almost daily discomfort." Four questions were raised from the Sabbatarian side: (1) How much proselytizing of others within the church was appropriate? (2) Could one still take communion with non-Sabbatarians? (3) How much loyalty did the Hubbard family owe to the church of Clarke and Holmes? (4) How should one behave toward those who became Sabbatarians and then changed their minds?[40]

It was that last question which forced a separation from the mother church. Two couples, Nicholas Wyld and John Salmon and their wives had been among the earliest to accept the Sabbath but early in 1669 they gave up the observance of the Seventh Day and even spoke out against it. The anxiety and discouragement which accompanied this "apostasy" as it was viewed is revealed in correspondence with the Sabbath keepers in England and with family members living in Westerly. To the church at Bell Lane in London, Hubbard wrote: "It is a very hard exercise to us, poor weak ones to lose four so suddenly out of the 11 of us here."[41] However, this

---

[39] This dating is taken from references to the signing of the covenant using the Old Style, or Julian calendar in use at the time which had the new year beginning in March. The new style or Gregorian calendar proposed in 1582 and currently in use begins on January 1, and omitted 10 days in October of that year with October 5th being called October 15th (There was no change in the sequence of the days of the week.) Thus December 23, 1671 was actually January 2, 1672 by modern reckoning. However, the actual decision to separate was December 7th which according to John Comer's document, was the time of the covenant. In which case the date according to the Julian or new style calendar would still be in 1671: December 17th, 1671.

[40] Edwin Gaustad, *Baptist Piety*, p. 52.

[41] Hubbard, Journal, p. 40 (3 July 1669)

25

apostasy alone would not have caused a separation were it not for other underlying differences.

Covenant and Communion: The concept of the covenant community was very strong in most of the New England churches of the time. In the Puritan churches of Massachusetts, the covenant was equivalent to citizenship in the state; one became a participating member of the state by being a participating member of the established church. In churches which practiced infant baptism, citizenship and membership were often assumed as a birthright for both state and church. However, as Kenneth Scott Latourette pointed out, the fathers who had brought the religious foundation to New England, did not always succeed in transmitting to their children and grandchildren their own experiences and convictions. The children of such members were baptized, but often because of a lack of any meaningful experience they could not become full members of a church. This led to what was nicknamed a *half-way covenant*.[42] They might receive one of the signs of a covenant, baptism, but unless they could present evidence of "regeneration" such persons could not participate in communion as the sign of the renewal of the covenant. One could not renew that which he had never experienced.

Baptists did not recognize any *half-way covenant*. Since baptism was only for believers, it was expected -- even demanded that the covenant be renewed in the sacrament of communion. This is one of the reasons why so many of the old church records are filled with attempts to discipline those members who had given evidence of a breaking of the covenant. They took seriously Christ's instructions about being reconciled to one's brother before going to the altar. They followed the three steps given in Matthew 18:15-17 to correct a broken covenant: first by personal confrontation, then by the testimony of two or three witnesses, and finally by taking the offense to the church body,[43]

William Hiscox, the Hubbards and the others who had arrived at the conviction of the Sabbath did not treat worship on the first day as a breaking of the covenant for those who had never made the Sabbath a part of their covenant conviction. But with those who had once accepted and then given it up, their covenant relationship was broken and they could no longer, in good conscience, share communion with the Baptist church in which the Wylds and Salmons were accepted. However, when they withdrew from the communion and held their own service on the Sabbath with Stephen and Ann Mumford, some like Obadiah Holmes and Joseph

---

[42] Kenneth Scott Latourette, *Three Centuries of Advance A. D. 1500-1800* (New York: Harper & Brothers, 1939) 192 - 193.

[43] Matthew 5:23-24 and 18:15-17.

Torrey in the Baptist Church interpreted this as a breaking of the Baptist Church covenant which brought them under discipline.

When called upon to give the reasons for not taking communion with the rest of the church, Tacy Hubbard gave three grounds: (1) the apostasy of the Wylds and Salmons who were still in good standing in the church; (2) the sermon of Obadiah Holmes in which he implied of the Sabbath keepers that "the offenses are such as arise from brethren in the church, such as deny Christ and have turned to Moses in observing days time and years, etc., and that it is better that a millstone were hanged about the neck of such, and they be cast into the sea;" and (3) "the dismal laying aside of the ten precepts, with the leading brethren denying them."[44]

Charges and Counter Charges: The differences within the church came to a head in 1671 following a series of sermons from the book of Galatians concerning the life in the Spirit apart from the law. Edwin Gaustad suggests that Obadiah Holmes became the catalyst in precipitating the final showdown in part as a means of strengthening his pastoral position in the church.[45] Yet there appears to have been a real fear that division could threaten the very existence of the church.

The church had already been racked by a split over the practice of laying-on-of-hands and other principles drawn from the sixth chapter of Hebrews. The rite of laying-on-of-hands traditionally had been reserved for ordination to the priesthood. Since Baptists affirmed the priesthood of all believers, some people believed that this act ought to be extended to all members at the time of baptism. Out of a church membership of less than fifty, twenty-one had withdrawn from the Newport First Baptist Church in 1656 to form a "Six Principle Baptist Church." Some of the fears of Holmes over the withdrawal of the Sabbath keepers were realized in the decades which followed. Only five removed their membership in 1671 over the Sabbath issue, but the "ripple effect" both in Newport and the westward expansion had its effect. By 1692 the list of members of the Sabbartarian church had grown to seventy-six while the mother church had declined to about 20 members. In 1694 that Baptist Church voted to place themselves for a time "under the ministry of the Rev. William Hiscox of the 7th day Church." Jonathan Holmes was one of those who voted for that move, "presumably with appropriate apologies to the memory of his father."[46] It should be noted however, that pastoral care extended to

---

[44] "The Newport Church" *Seventh Day Baptist Memorial* (New York: Seventh Day Baptist Publishing Society 1852-54) vol. 1: 1 p. 34.

[45] Gaustad, *Baptist Piety* p. 53-54.

[46] Gaustad, *Baptist Piety* p. 106. (from Newport Historical Society Vault A, Box 50 Folder 5.

preaching and certain other services to the church, but it did not extend to the serving of communion. For this sacrament, pastors from other Baptist communities visited Newport. The importance of the communion covenant remained a non-negotiable.[47] It seems ironic that one of the charges levied against William Hiscox was that "you have not Conscience toward God in the matter of the Sabbath; for if you had; you could not have walked so long with the church as you have done."[48]

An extended text of the debate which took place in the Baptist Church has been preserved in the record book of the First Baptist Church, but it can only be summarized here. After a protracted series of meetings and debate with attempts of a number of the congregation including Dr. John Clarke to reach some kind of agreement, the situation became critical for both segments of the church. In a declaration to the church, Obadiah Holmes summarized charges against the Sabbathkeepers. (1) Brother Hiscox slandered the leading brethren in saying they deny the law. (2) He had charged four persons as Apostates, adding that in his judgment the church ought to make Brother Hiscox see his evil in charging them so highly or else that the church ought to look at them as such and declare against them. (3) It was reported that Brother Hiscox did work one first day till meeting time and then came and stood up in the church to speak and pray. (4) He had broken bread on the 7th day of the week. (5) That in so doing, he held communion with such as were not owned by the church. (Those who were not owned by the church would have been Stephen and Ann Mumford.) Holmes then called upon the church to deal with Mr. Hiscox for these great evils.

William Hiscox accepted the challenge, saying that he was glad to speak of such things, for he had heard that Holmes or some others had "spake of such things abroad, but not to me." As to the first charge, he replied, "If I have slandered the leading brethren in saying they have denied the law or the Ten Words to be a rule unto us Gentiles, I have said and I do

---

[47] A similar position was demonstrated in 1726, when the First Baptist Church invited the Seventh Day Baptists to assist in the ordination of John Comer. Although they had shared worship and often preached in their pulpit, participating in ordination, like communion, was within a covenant relationship and so they responded, "We Believe your neglect to observe the fourth Commandment is a Just objection that we cannot grant your Request." cited in McLoughlin, New England Dissent, 1630-1833 Vol. I p. 308-309. Backus Papers, Rhode Island Historical Society vol. 1 pg. 5 , cf. SDB Historical Society ms. 189.32.1-2.

[48] From Typescript copy of "excerpts from the Newport First Baptist Church Book Describing Differences with Seventh Day Baptists in 1671 p. 4.

say so still. And if Brother Holmes or any other do deny it, their last sin could be as bad as their first, having said it publicly and privately. Should they deny it, it would be only adding sin to sin." As to the second charge of calling the four persons apostates, he said, "We can look upon them no better, for what is apostasy but the denial in a back way of that which persons once professed to be the mind and will of God? Would not you count us as such if we should deny water baptism and turn our backs upon it and plead for a baptism of the Spirit only -- as too, too many do at this day?"

At this point Joseph Torrey responded, "If apostasy be to deny that which persons once professed, then most of the church are apostates." To which Hiscox replied, "Look you to that, if you have done anything in the name of the Lord and have forsook it, whether you have need to repent of it." Hiscox then turned to the third charge as he denied ever coming from work to speak and pray in the church, but once, many years ago on a more than ordinary occasion when Brother Clarke was sick. Then William Hiscox took the offensive, and said, "I cannot but wonder at you, Brother Holmes, of whom I heard before I saw your face that you could as freely weave a yard or two of cloth of the First Day, before meeting as at any other time." When challenged as to whether he had ever seen him do it, Hiscox replied, "No, but I have seen you come to meeting on a First Day with your leather apron on, as if you came from your work, which make me think it might be true, especially hearing you ofttimes say you had no Sabbath but Christ." By that time Hiscox never had a chance to answer charges four and five since there was "so much disorder in the meeting that the other things were not spoke to."[49] The proceedings thus reached a point of no return and separation was inevitable.

The separation did not take place in haste or without consultation with others. The three positions exhibited earlier in the trial of Thomas Goold were reflected in advice given to the five who eventually separated. In 1671 Thomas Goold traveled to Newport to consult with the Sabbatarians and urged them to stay within the church "and get along with them as they could."[50] The second position of holding parallel communion is found in a 1670 letter to Edward Stennett of London.

> Having declared by one for all that we cannot have full
> freedom of spirit with those that are fallen back from the truth
> once professed, most do hold yet full communion in breaking of
> bread, & the rest of the ordinance with them. But this by grace
> we are helped to do, we in our measure endeavor to sanctify

---

49 Transcript of Excerpts from the *Church Book* p. 8-9.
50 Gaustad, *Baptist Piety* p. 53 from Newport Historical Society, Vault A, Box 50) Folder 3, Wood pp. 108-109.

God's holy sabbath by assembling ourselves for us to pray and edify each other, and no man disturbs us in any kind: Blessed be God.[51]

A previous letter from Stennett asserted the third position of complete independence as he referred to the four apostates as having the same spirit of antichrist as had afflicted the church in London. He urged them to withdraw from them "as sinful and disorderly persons; & if your church will hold communion with those apostates...ye ought then to withdraw yourselves, & not be partakers of other men's sins, but keep your elves pure with all humility, meekness & brokenness of heart."[52]

Thus on December 7, 1671, the final separation was made, though it was about two weeks later that the covenant was signed by the five who separated along with Stephen and Ann Mumford. The third Baptist Church in Newport became a reality even though cordial relations continued and many of the old personal ties remained intact.

---

[51] Letter, September 4, 1670 signed by the five plus Stephen Mumford, Hubbard *Journal* p. 60-61.

[52] Letter from Abingdon January 6 1669/70, Hubbard *Journal.*, p. 56

Chapter 4

A MEETING HOUSE FOR WORSHIP

There are no known records which tell where the members of the newly organized church of Sabbath keepers met for worship. Presumably they met in the home of one or more of their members, but as their numbers increased an individual dwelling might have become crowded. However, since a sizable proportion of the membership lived in Westerly (Hopkinton) and various other locations the actual congregation at Newport was never large. In 1708 about seventy-two members were set off as an independent church in Westerly although the record book continues as though the churches were one body meeting alternately for communion at the two locations.

Charles H. Greene suggested that the church may have met for a time at Green End where a chapel was erected and jointly owned by the evangelical churches of Newport.[53] Mrs. Gladys Bolhouse, former curator of the Newport Historical Society, stated that the first church on the Island of Rhode Island of which we have actual record was at Green End in Middletown. The early records of the Baptist church tell of meeting there, although it may have been more of a "baptizing house" rather than an actual meeting house.[54] The first mention in the Seventh Day Baptist records of a meeting at Green End appears in 1753. "We had a meeting at the meeting house at Green End where Mr. Thomas Hiscox preached an excellent sermon from Luke 6:46. After the sermon, Richard Ward, Esq. was baptized and passed under the ordinance of hands and was received into the church."[55] The record book continues with many other services of baptism at this location. At a church meeting in 1765 Samuel Green was appointed "to join with others as shall be appointed by the other Baptist Churches to confer and agree what proportion each church shall pay towards the repair of the meeting house at Green End and to agree what repairs shall be made."[56] Four years later William Bliss was appointed to join other representatives in repairing the meeting house at Green End. This suggests joint responsibility if not joint ownership. During the Revolutionary War this meeting house fell into disrepair and was demolished soon after its conclusion.

---

[53] Charles H. Greene, "History of Seventh Day Baptists in America, Newport, Rhode Island" unpublished manuscript, p. 28-29.

[54] Gladys Bolhouse "Old Churches of Newport" ms. p. 1.

[55] Hand script copy of the *Newport Church Records* copied by Joseph Stillman from the original 1834. p. 201-202.

[56] Newport Church Records, p. 209.

The First Meeting House: In 1706 a deed was executed from Jonathan Barney for property extending forty feet on what is now Spring Street and eighty-five 85 feet along Barney Street on which a church building could be erected. The deed was made out to Arnold Collins, a goldsmith and a member of the congregation at a cost of "twenty-one pounds, six shillings and eight pence current passable money at eight shillings per ounce silver."[57] On this lot a meeting house about seventeen feet by twenty-six feet was erected. Two years later an additional lot was purchased to the southeast, thirty feet along Barney St.

According to the deed records of 1712, Arnold Collins on behalf of the church sold a house and lot from the original purchase on the corner of Spring and Barney Street to Joseph Bennett for one hundred pounds. Within that document there is the record of an exclusion from the deed of sale "for ever hereinafter the House called and known by ye name of ye Seventh Day Baptist Meeting house and Land whereon the same is now erected and built." It granted passage around the building for "mending and repairing" as well as protecting the windows from shading or darkening by Joseph Bennett or his heirs.[58] This reference is the first known legal document which uses the term Seventh Day Baptist in the identification of the church. A few years later when consideration was given to the sale of further land the document was read at a 1718 church meeting, "in order that the church or congregation of Seventh Day Baptists may have full authority to claim challenge and demand all rites and profit arising ..."[59] The church minutes thus also verify that the members thought of themselves as Seventh Day Baptists even though the popular term *Sabbatarian* was still frequently used.

The Second Meeting House: At a church meeting held on November 9, 1729 the following action was taken:

> Voted that Jonathan Weeden and Henry Collins take a deed of Mr. Job Almy of the land on the backside of the meeting house for the use of the Church and be appointed Trustees to take a deed in their names for the use of the Church aforesaid.
>
> Voted that a meeting house be Built 36 feet in length and 26 feet in Breadth on part of the land wherein their present meeting house now stands.

---

[57] From original deed in possession of the Seventh Day Baptist Historical Society, CRR 1993.1

[58] Land Evidence Records, Vol. 1, p. 39 Newport Historical Collection.

[59] Newport Church minutes April 29, 1718.

Voted at the same time that Jonathan Weeden and Henry Collins be appointed a committee to undertake in the whole affair of erecting said house and to raise the money by subscription.

Voted at the same time that the two above mentioned brethren do their endeavor to make sale of their present meeting house to the best advantage they can and dispose of the money towards the better finishing the house they are to erect.[60]

It is quite probable that the congregation met in the old Baptist church on Tanner Street (now West Broadway) during the period of construction of the meeting house. In 1730 John Comer, the pastor of the Baptist Church, records several times in his diary that on Saturday "the 7th Day Congregation met in my old Meeting House." Comer also wrote that when Pastor Crandall was sick, "I preached in my old meeting house to his congregation." Other references show that there was considerable exchange of pulpit with Thomas Hiscox and Joseph Crandall preaching for Comer's congregation, and Comer preaching for the Seventh Day Baptists. Near the end of June 1730, Comer recorded: "The 7th day meeting house was raised this day."[61]

In 1738 when the city was celebrating its centennial, the pastor of the Baptist Church, John Calender, preached his century sermon in the Seventh Day Baptist Meeting House since their new church was under construction. For nearly three centuries this practice of sharing facilities and pastoral services has existed among Seventh Day Baptists.[62] With their services on the seventh day, Sunday was thus free for sharing with others the basic theologies and ideals upon which there was little difference.

C. H. Greene described the 1729 meeting house as being "a plain frame structure, without steeple or exterior ornament of any sort, 36 x 25 feet in size, with high pulpit perched like a swallow's nest up on the wall, with a large ornamented sounding board descending above it. The house was furnished with substantial box pews, with sides sufficiently high to keep the eyes of a heedless congregation from roving carelessly about the room. Around three sides of the building were substantial galleries; on the west wall above the pulpit hung the tablets of the law, written in gilt, a most ornate piece of workmanship." The tablets of law were not added to the pulpit area

---

[60] Microfilm copy of *Newport, R. I. SDB Church Records, 1708-1817* (SDB Historical Society, Janesville WI CRR 1980.12) p. 78.

[61] Manuscript of John Comer's Diary, Rhode Island Historical Society Library C 732 ms 5, notes by Janet Thorngate.

[62] A branch of the Newport Church located at New London, Connecticut (Waterford) SDB Church met in private homes until 1710 when a Meeting House was erected in conjunction with the First Day Baptists, and was used by both societies until 1816.

until 1773 when John Tanner had the Ten Commandments in letters of gold put up in the pulpit at a cost of twenty-five dollars.

The plain unadorned exterior structure was typical of most of the separatist churches of the time which rebelled against the elaborate cathedrals of the Church of England which had retained many of the trappings of Catholicism. As late as 1769 Ezra Stiles who, prior to becoming the President of Yale University was the Congregational minister in Newport, wrote in his diary, "the baptists have no bell, they would as soon have a crucifix as a bell on their church."[63] On the other hand, the pulpit was architecturally significant for it was the focal point of evangelical Christianity. It was here that the preaching took place and the word was proclaimed.

The Preservation Cooperative report of 1993 called the interior "one of the finest early 18th century interiors in Rhode Island and is richly decorated with paneling and bolection moulding. The wineglass pulpit is reached by a flight of beautiful stairs with turned, carved and twisted balusters."[64] George Mason in *The American Architecture and Building News* of 1885 described the stairs as partaking of the characteristic features of the best domestic work of the day, but "are richer in detail and more delicately wrought than any other staircase of the time."[65] There is a striking similarity of this pulpit to that of Trinity Church built in 1726 leading many to believe that Richard Munday designed both.

The old meeting house had twenty four box pews on two levels. The main floor had four in a cluster in the center, four along the west wall, three along the east wall, one on the right of the pulpit against the north wall, and one on either side of the front entrance. The one to the right as one entered was reserved for strangers. In the gallery there were four smaller boxes along the railing on the west end, three along the middle section and three along the east gallery railing. The stairway occupied the southeast corner of the meeting house. There is no known record of the names of the pew holders, but as indicated in the reminiscence of Maude Howe Elliott, the Ward family had its pew and other prominent families followed the common practice of renting or even buying their pew space. One report indicates that the pews "in the east gallery were occupied by the colored people."[66] The church records contain

---

[63] cited by Gladys Bolhouse "Old Churches of Newport" ms. p. 1.

[64] Preservation Cooperative report 1993 , "The Seventh Day Baptist \ Sabbatarian Meeting House 1929" p. 5.

[65] George Mason, "The Seventh Day Baptist Church of Newport, R. I.," The American Architect and Building News vol. XVIII No. 488 May 2, 1885 p. 211 Cited in Preservation Cooperative report 1993 p. 14

[66] James M. K. Southwick, chairman of the Improvement Committee in his address at the dedication of the Meeting House as the as the

the names of a number of Negroes and Indians who were baptized and accepted as full members of the church.

Although C. H. Greene may have viewed the box pews as advantageous for keeping one's eyes focused on the pulpit, their primary advantage was conservation of heat. Few churches had centralized heating, so each family brought its foot warmers or metal boxes filled with live coals. A boxed in pew preserved the heat. (It also provided a sanctuary for children who might find diverse amusement or even fall asleep during the normal two hour sermon.) "Long and tedious must have been the sermons in former years," wrote Mrs. R. Sherman Elliott, "for even today may be plainly seen initials carved in the railing. This was not because the pastor lacked knowledge of the fleeting hours, for there before his very eyes hung the clock made by William Claggett, a worthy member of the Sabbatarian congregation in 1731, and an excellent clock maker of that period."[67] That clock to this day still hangs on the center balcony railing.

The Revolutionary War had considerable effect upon the churches of Newport. As a leading seaport in New England, with an exceptionally good harbor, the British were quick to occupy the harbor and the island. In addition to its strategic military value, the British found many supporters among the aristocracy who were dependent upon trade for their economic and cultural interests. Trinity Church was forced to close after the British evacuated Newport at the close of the war because many of the members of the Episcopal, or Church of England were loyalists and left with the British troops, never to return. Several of the other churches were used by the British as barracks or hospitals. Some were even used as stables for horses. The Seventh Day Baptist Meeting House was not disturbed. Tradition holds that the church was spared because of the presence of the Ten Commandments behind the pulpit and the design on the underside of the sounding board which resembled the Union Jack. Others believe that several prominent members of the congregation, such as John Tanner, were more sympathetic to the British than the American cause.[68]

Quarters for the Newport Historical Society, November 10, 1884, printed in the *Newport Mercury* newspaper November 15, 1884.

[67] Mrs. R. Sherman Elliott, "The Seventh Day Baptists Meeting House" A paper read before the Newport Historical Society November 18, `1929 and printed in the Society's Bulletin January 1930.

[68] A stone in the cemetery at Hopkinton reads: "Here lies the dust of Mrs. Mary Tanner wife of John Tanner, esq. of Newport Rhode Island, who to escape the Storm and dangers of an unnatural and cruel Civil War, took refuge in a rural retreat......"

Yet though the meeting house may have escaped damage, the congregation suffered greatly and declined following the war. Many who were loyal to the Colonial cause, fled to the mainland. Those who stayed, suffered from the quartering of soldiers and their demands upon resources and business. The end of the war opened up avenues to the frontier regions of New York, Pennsylvania, western Virginia and the Old Northwest Territory. Many of these churches still list descendants of the Newport Seventh Day Baptist Church on their rolls.

The post Revolutionary War period saw a change in the fortunes and character of both the church and Newport society. The church continued its regular appointments recording its minutes until 1836. A continuation was begun in 1843 with the note: "It will be seen by the records of our church, that from March 1836 to May 1843, a period of seven years, we did no business as a church or in other words had no church meeting during that time... Yet at the same time so far as the declining years and health of our Elder Henry Burdick would allow, Sabbath worship was continued."[69] The initial reason for the resumed meeting dealt with the formation of a Missionary Compact with other New England churches of the faith. However, much of the business recorded revolved around problems involved with the use of the meeting house by the Fourth Baptist Church of Newport.

In 1840 the Trustees of the Fourth Baptist Church were assigned the task of locating a suitable place to meet for public worship. Of this action, Mrs. Elliott reported:

> They have obtained liberty of the Trustees of the Sabbatarian meeting house to have it under the following conditions, viz.: that the Church by paying thirty-five dollars per year in repairs upon said Sabbatarian Meeting House may have it at any time and at all times except Saturdays for to hold meetings in except the Sabbatarian Society would wish to occupy it for a special meeting and then they would give timely notice to the 4th Baptist Church.[70]

It probably would have been far better had the agreement been in a straight specified rent unrelated to repairs, for the lack of accountability created troubles which persisted for a dozen years. It was not until 1855 that the matter was finally resolved. The following year the trustees reported:

> After much labor and long delay we obtained from the Trustees of the Fourth Baptist Church an offer to give up their lease for two hundred and fifty dollars, if the money was paid them by the first of

---

[69] "Continuation of the Records of the Seventh Day Baptist Church of Newport, R I. 1843-1872 p. 1. (CRR 1922 SDB Historical Society)

[70] Mrs. R. Sherman Elliott, "The Seventh Day Baptist Meeting House" Bulletin of the Newport Historical Society No. 73 January 1930.

December 1855. This offer was obtained in August preceding. We then made efforts to raise the money, and succeeded, so that we paid the amount required, and the lease was removed from the property, and the same made a matter of record in the Town Clerk's office at Newport."[71]

During this long interlude the church also made efforts to incorporate. Beginning in May 1846, the minutes show several delays in the process, but do not indicate that the final steps were taken. However, at a special meeting of the church on June 5th 1872 a meeting was held in which the Board of Trustees was enlarged to include representatives of the Hopkinton Church. This new board was then instructed "to ascertain if our Church is now empowered to hold, possess or convey Real Estate or other property. And if not to take measure to secure the Church said rights." It also instructed the trustees "to make disposition of the Meeting House and Lot, by sale or otherwise as in their judgment shall be thought best." At that same meeting, the treasurer was instructed "to inquire after and relieve as far as he reasonably can, the necessities or wants of any of our aged or needy members." The final action of the church body was a vote that "in case the Meeting House is sold the Clock and Tables of Law shall be reserved from sale, and taken care of as the church may direct -- or in the absence of instructions as the Trustees may think best.[72]

There is no mention in the available minutes of the church to what Mrs. Elliott reported concerning the use of the meeting house by the Shiloh Baptist Church from 1864 to 1869. She reported that it was at this time that supports were placed under the balcony, with the added note: "to those of you who have attended a New Year's Eve revival meeting of an animated Ethiopian congregation there is no need to explain the need of extra supports."[73]

Newport Historical Society Ownership: The opportunity for sale of the old meeting house was realized in 1884 when the Newport Historical Society was looking for a suitable facility for their meetings and the preservation of their growing collections of historic artifacts. At the formal dedication of the meeting house as the Newport Historical Society Library Mr. James Southwick, chairman of the Improvement Committee, reported that after looking at all the places suggested, they unanimously recommended the purchase of the meeting house "as being the most practical on account of

---

[71] from "Minutes of the Newport SDB Church 1843-1872."

[72] The final entry in the minute book is that of a Trustee meeting on June 7, 1872 which empowered John Congdon to be Chairman of the Board and Acting Trustee to implement the action of the church and to see that safe keeping of all the records of the church be provided.

[73] Elliott, "the Seventh Day Baptist Meeting House" p. 12.

the low price at which it could be obtained, the general interest felt in this historic building, the interesting relics it possessed and its adaptability to the purposes of the Society."[74]

On June 24, 1884 a deed was granted and the work of restoration began, for time had taken its toll on the 155 year old structure. Mr. Southwick described some of the initial work in reconstruction.

> First it became necessary to straighten the building, which by reason of rotted sills had settled a foot or more to the rear or north. The sides also were bulged out at the plate, compelling the use of three iron rods to draw it in and keep it in place. Before raising the building, which is six inches higher than it ever was before, an entire new sill had to be put in and an entire new floor frame had to follow; not a piece of the old wood was used except a short piece of red cedar timber running from the door to midway of the house and supporting the sleepers.[75]

Mrs. Elliott reported other work which included the removal of the old pews to be used as wainscoating around the room, thus making the paneling that you see now and preserving what remained of the original pews; the rebuilding of the foundation wall and resetting the steps. After the building was in place came the repair of the roof. "The shingles were blown from the old one so that the light of heaven came to reveal more clearly the ruin, but more copiously came the rain to make the ruin sure and speedy."[76] The solid oak frame and the heavy oak trusses that supported the roof were saved, but the rafters and the 4" x 4" fur pieces to which the ceiling laths were attached had to be replaced. The window frames and much of the clapboard exterior were also replaced. The west end had its original covering of clapboard which needed to be replaced, but as Mr. Southwick reported, "Our neighbor had so crowded his building up to us on that side that it seemed a mystery how this was to be accomplished in so narrow a space, and we can hardly account for it; but be that as it may, it is true the new clap-boards are there with two coats of paint on them."[77]

---

[74] James M. K. Southwick, paper presented at the dedication of the building to the Newport Historical Society, reprinted in *Newport Mercury* vol. 127:22 November 15, 1884.

[75] Southwick, *loc. cit.*

[76] Elliott, "The Seventh Day Baptist Meeting House" *Newport Historical Society Bulletin,* January 1930, p. 13. (Some of her quotes were from Southwick's address.)

[77] Southwick, *loc. cit.* quoted by Edith May Tilley, *The Newport Historical Society in its Earlier Days,* NHS Bulletin No. 12 April 1914, p. 10 and cited in Preservation Cooperative Report 1993 p. 8.

Although great care was taken to preserve the interior appearance, much of the exterior had no distinguishing features and resembled many other buildings of its time. Thus it was decided to make some changes which would give it more the appearance of a public building and at the same time add to its historic value. The caps over the front windows did not match for they were taken from two older buildings that had been built in the previous century. The bow window over the front door had once graced an apothecary shop which had been built in 1794.

Dedication: On November 10, 1884 the old meeting house was formally dedicated. James Southwick in presenting the keys to the president of the Newport Historical Society refers to the whole project as a labor of love, recalling: "our earliest associations cluster around this house; in 1762, my great-grandfather joined the church that then worshipped here; my father was a member of another church that leased this house in 1840; my namesake preached from this pulpit; I was taught the word of God by a Christian lady, now living, in one of the pews we found here, and it was here I was received into the church, having for its creed, the inspired Word of God as handed down to us." Alfred D. Burdick, a deacon from the Hopkinton Seventh Day Baptist Church gave a response saying:

> While we deeply regret the necessity which there seemed to be for the sale of the building, we cannot feel as though this had been a lost cause. The work still goes on; the funds received from the sale of this building go into a permanent fund, the proceeds of which will be used for mission purposes; that this ancient building, so dear to us, with that tablet of Commandments which saved it from destruction by the British soldiers in the time of the Revolutionary War; this pulpit, in which so many of God's servants have stood and broken to many generations the Bread of Life; this clock which has given the time of day to so many thousands --- and we do not today regret that they have passed into the hands of the Newport Historical Society, to some of whom of the membership of which we know this is also sacred ground and will be well cared for.[78]

Newport Historical Society Use: The local newspaper at the time of the dedication.reported that the hall presented a handsome appearance, and must have been a great surprise to those who saw it for the first time since the improvements were made. "The librarian, Mr. R. H. Tilley, had tastefully

---

[78] Alfred B. Burdick 2nd, Response at the Dedication Service November 10 1884, printed in the *Newport Mercury*, vol. 127:22 November 15, 1884.

arranged the numerous possessions of the Society about the room. The walls were hung with pictures of more or less historical significance and the various bookcases were well filled with volumes and records pertaining to the early history of Newport and Newporters; the whole bespeaking in unmistakable language, the character of the place."[79]

Having a facility of its own stimulated growth of the Historical Society and its holdings. Yet with growth came growing pains. Almost from the beginning there was concern over the safety and particularly the inflammability of the building and its collection. Of particular concern was the proximity of a blacksmith shop, a carriage shop, several stables and even a paint shop, all of which posed threat to the safety of the Historical Society holdings. In 1887 a lot was purchased on Touro Street next to the Jewish synagogue which had been built in 1763. The task of moving was hampered by the closeness of neighboring buildings. It was found that the overhanging jets did not leave room to get through the street, but with an occasional rub, the move across Barney Street to the middle of the new lot was accomplished. "The building started from its original site Nov. 23, 1887 at just 3 p.m. It was over the cellar on the new site Nov. 26, 1887 (Saturday evening). On Tuesday Dec. 6, the new corner stone was put in place and the building was let down onto the foundation." [80]

The new lot gave room for needed expansion, thus in 1889 an addition was added to the rear of the meeting house for the Newport Natural History Society. This addition measured 45' x 26', more than doubled the floor space and provided a separate entrance. As the holdings of the Historical Society increased in both volume and value, the need for more space and security became evident. Ground was broken in 1902 for a brick library building on the Touro Street side of the lot. The new building provided office space for the Society, fire proof vaults for the preservation of records and a library for research. Visitors today still use this entrance into the whole historical complex. A passageway with a fire door connected the library with the meeting house at the rear.

A decade later the Historical Society again suffered growing pains. In 1915 the Natural History addition was removed; the meeting house was again moved, this time to the rear of the lot close to Barney Street, but still facing the library and Touro Street. A three story brick building was then constructed between the library and the meeting house. It was at this time that the brick veneer, a state roof and steel shutters were added to the exterior of the meeting house to make its exterior covering consistent with the adjoining structures, to give added protection from the weather as well as

---

[79] *Newport Mercury* loc. cit.

[80] Recording Secretary notes of the Newport Historical Society as reported in the Preservation Cooperative 1993 report. p. 10.

the threat of fire in a highly flammable environment. As the meeting house approached its 250th anniversary in 1979 extensive painting and some repair work was done, the metal roof was recoated and the shutters were replaced, but the basic structure had withstood the test of time. In 1993 when the Preservation Cooperative did its extensive analysis, it validated the forethought of those who had given such care to the preservation of one of Newport's most significant structures. The Preservation Cooperative concluded its historical sketch with these words:

> While contemporary students of history, architecture and historic preservation would adhere to a different philosophy in the preservation of the building on its original site and maintaining its original exterior fabric, the forethought and caring of the NHS in the preservation of this structure is to be applauded.

The Seventh Day Baptist / Sabbatarian Meeting House, encased in its brick exterior, remains in the care of the Newport Historical Society more than a century after the deed passed into their hands. The Society recognized the significance of this outstanding architectural interior and the contribution that the original congregation made to the history of Newport.[81]

---

[81] Preservation Cooperative report p. 11

Chapter 5
Seventh Day Baptists in Newport Society

The Seventh Day Baptist Meeting House is significant not only for its architectural interior but also as a reminder of the importance that its members had in Newport, Rhode Island and American history. As the Preservation Cooperative report stated: "This beautiful and architecturally significant interior was and is a symbol of the wealth, education and talent of the congregation's distinguished members."[82] Not all of the members had wealth or were educated, for there were numbered among its members several Indians and servants of color who at that time would have been denied many of the privileges of society. But there was a significant number of members who helped shape the culture of Newport and beyond. The 1655 list of those with status of Freemen in the colony who were given the right to vote included such names from Newport as, Benedict Arnold (not to be confused with his namesake of Reveloutionary fame), James Barker, Joseph Clarke, John Crandall, Edward Greenman, Samuel Hubbard, James Rogers, Tobias Saunders, and Andrew Langworthy, all of whom later became members of the Seventh Day Baptist Church. Their early involvement was carried on by later generations in helping to shape the character and distinguishing marks of Newport and Rhode Island political, educational, economic, social, and religious life.

Political Leadership: The first President of the Colony to succeed Roger Williams was Benedict Arnold. He served two terms 1657-1660 and 1662-1663. After the new charter was granted by Charles II in 1663, Arnold served three terms as Rhode Island's first governor (1663-1666, 1669-1672, and 1677- 1678). Although his name is not found on any of the existing records of the Newport Church, there is strong evidence that he was a member. William Hiscox was his pastor during his final illness and preached his funeral sermon at his death in 1678. The Arnold name is found on the membership roll of the Newport Church.[83] Other members of the

---

[82] Preservation Cooperative Report 1993 p. 5

[83] One of the descendents, James Arnold, claims that Benedict Arnold (not the traitor of a later generation) was a Seventh Day Baptist. It is reported that Gov. Arnold called for Elder Hiscox to be with him at his death, calling for him even during a Sabbath service. Several family members are on the 1692 roll of the church. in printring the list of members

43

Sabbatarian church and its branches at Hopkinton and Westerly served in public office on both state and local level including governors, secretary of state, legislators, commissioners, and members of the court. Evidence of the influence of the Sabbatarians in Newport on a day to day basis was the adding of a new market day, Thursday of each week, to the old market day on Saturday, mainly to accommodate the Sabbath-keepers. This was done in 1677, just six years after the organization of the Seventh Day Baptist Church.[84]

The Ward Family: The most politically prominent Seventh Day Baptist family in Newport was the family of Thomas Ward who came to Newport in 1671. In 1677 he was elected General Treasurer of the Colony. Two years later he was elected to the upper house of the General Assembly, equivalent to a modern senator and was repeatedly chosen a Deputy from Newport until his death in 1689 at age of 48. It is not known when he joined the Seventh Day Baptist Church, but his name appears on the membership list of 1692 when the second record book begins. His oldest daughter by his first wife was Mary who became the wife of Sion Arnold, the son of Gov. Benedict Arnold. Mary joined the church in 1704. Thomas Ward's contribution to Rhode Island extended beyond his political career. His gifts to the Redwood Library reveals the broad scope of his interests. Among the books he donated from his own library were, *A Greek and Latin edition of Dionysius* (1688), *The Origin and Institution of Civil Government Discussed by Hoadly* (1710), *Keill's Introductio ad Veram Astronomiam*, and John Calvin's *Institutio Christianae Religionis*[85] Upon his death, his widow married Arnold Collins thus linking the Ward family with Henry Collins of which more will be written.

The second wife of Thomas Ward was Amy Smith, a granddaughter of Roger Williams. Her name also appears on the 1692 list of church members. To this union two sons were born, Thomas, Jr. who died at the age of 12, and Richard who continued in his father's footsteps. Richard Ward was for

---

as of that date, the note is made, "the loss of the first book of records probably has deprived us of the knowledge of some names of persons who may have died previous to the before-mentioned date, and therefore not on the list with which the second volume commences" *SDB Memorial* vol 1 no. 3 July 1852, p. 121.

[84] C. H. Greene, Newport Manuscript, p. 23 citing S. G. Arnold, The History of Rhode Island.

[85] George Champlin Mason, *Annals of the Redwood Library and Athenaeum* (Redwood Library, Newport RI 1891) footnote p. 11.

many years the Secretary of the Colony and afterwards Governor from 1740 to 1743.[86] His report to the English Board of Trade on paper money written in 1740 provides a good summary of the economics of the Colony in relation to the British crown.[87] His wife, Mary, joined the Seventh Day Baptist Church in 1714 but Richard delayed his baptism and membership until 1753. At his death in 1763, a legacy was given to the church to be applied toward the purchase of a house for the use of the church.

Richard and Mary had fourteen children, five of whom died at ages of three years or less. Three of their sons went on to public service, while a daughter, Elizabeth became the second wife of Rev. William Bliss, the fifth pastor of the Newport Church. The oldest son, Thomas, was for many years Secretary of State for the colony until his death in 1760, at which time he was succeeded by his youngest brother, Henry, who was reelected annually until his death in 1797. The other son, Samuel was the most illustrious of all. His early years were spent in Newport where he worshipped in the old Ward family pew. His membership, however, was with the First Hopkinton Seventh Day Baptist Church which he joined in 1769, followed by his wife, two daughters and a sister in 1770. His letter dated August 5, 1769 to the church is preserved and gives a testimony of his faith:

To the Sabbatarian Church of Christ in Westerly & Hopkinton:

Being fully satisfied that Baptism is a Christian Duty I desire to be admitted to that Ordinance this Day: my Life & Conversation are well known: my religious Sentiments are That there is one God the Father of whom are all Things and one Lord Jesus Christ by whom are all Things, That the Universe thus created has been preserved and governed by infinite Wisdom, Power and Goodness from the Beginning. That mankind having fallen into the most gross & unnatural Idolatry, Superstition and Wickedness it pleased God for their Recovery to make a Revelation of his mind & will in the holy Scriptures which (excepting the ceremonial Law and some part of the Judicial Law peculiar to the Jews) It is the Duty of all mankind to whom they are made known sincerely to believe and obey: My Sins I sincerely & heartily repent of and firmly rely upon the unbounded Goodness and Mercy of God in his only begotten Son Christ Jesus for Pardon & eternal Life: and I sincerely desire and Resolve by his Grace for the future to walk in all the Commandments and Ordinances of the Lord.[88]

---

[86]   John Ward, A Genealogy of the Ward Family, in A Memoir of Lieut. Colonel Samuel Ward (NewYork 1875) p. 15-16

[87]   reprinted in John Russell Bartlett's *Records of the Colony of Rhode Island and Providence Plantations in New England,* vol 5, p. 8-14.

[88] Original in possession of the SDB. Hist. Soc. Janesville

Samuel Ward did not have the benefit of higher education since his father had prepared him for the life of a farmer.[89] His wife, Anne Ray, was also a descendent of Roger Williams and a daughter of a prominent farmer on Block Island. Soon after their marriage the couple settled on a farm in Westerly. His first appearance in public affairs came as a representative from the town of Westerly in the General Assembly of Rhode Island. From that point his service elevated to the governorship of the colony during the turbulent years leading to the Revolutionary War. He was the only one of the thirteen colonial governors to refuse to sign the Stamp Act. He established in each community in Rhode Island a committee of intelligence to secure information on the British movements.

In 1774 he was chosen to represent the colony at the First Continental Congress. The following year he returned for the Second Continental Congress where he served as chairman of the Committee as a Whole, recommended George Washington for Commander-in-Chief and fought hard for the establishment of a colonial navy. His death in March of 1776 prevented him from signing the Declaration of Independence for which he had ardently worked. His body was interred in Philadelphia, but in 1860 his descendants had his remains moved to the old Newport Burial Grounds where it rests next to that of his father beneath a stone bearing a tribute to his life.

Seventh Day Baptists and Brown University: Any lack of formal education did not deter Samuel Ward from support of higher education. While governor he signed the charter establishing Rhode Island University which later became Brown University. Walter Bronson in his History of Brown University expressed the need which the Baptists felt for a college of their own.

"If the Baptist denomination was to work out its destiny under God, and get an educated ministry the Baptists must have schools and colleges of their own: first, because Baptist youth, living for four years in a college atmosphere strongly charged with influences hostile to their faith, might cease to be Baptists, or at least become lukewarm; and, secondly, because many Baptists were indifferent or

---

[89]Some biographeies list him as having graduated from Harvard in 1773, but Harvard has no record of his attending. "His father was at the head of a large commercial and agricultural interest at Newport where Samuel cquired an extensive knowledge of the duties of a merchant and a farmer." *Records of the Colony of Rhode Island*, ed. Bartlett, Vol. VII 170-176.

even averse to higher education, and could best be won over by means of institutions controlled by their own sect."[90]

The establishment of this college in Rhode Island was a decision of the Philadelphia Association and Baptists throughout the thirteen colonies who recognized that Rhode Island was the only state which had a majority of Baptists in the legislature. Seventh Day Baptists from both Newport and Hopkinton were among the strongest supporters in the establishment of a Baptist college. Col. Job Bennett, a judge of the superior court, was one of the drafters of the charter and served on the Board of Trustees from its beginning to his death in 1784. He also served as its treasurer from 1767 to 1775. Other Seventh Day Baptists on the first Board of Trustees in addition to Ward and Bennett were Rev. John Maxson of Newport (1764 - 1778) and Joshua Clarke of Hopkinton (1764 - 1789). John Tanner of the Newport Church was added to the Board in 1768 serving until his death in 1785, while Pastor William Bliss served from 1785 to 1793. Dr. Joshua Babcock of the Hopkinton Church served from 1764 to 1783 on the Board of Fellows, the body which was charged with the academic affairs of the College.[91]

The charter for Brown University specified that of the thirty-six trustees, twenty-two "shall forever be elected of the Denomination called Baptists, or Antipaedobaptists, Five shall forever be elected of the Denomination called Friends, or Quakers; Four shall forever be elected of the Denomination called Congregationalists and Five shall forever be elected of the Denomination called Episcopalians: And that the Succession in this Branch shall be forever chosen and filled up from the respective Denominations in this Proportion, and according to these Numbers; which are hereby fixed and shall remain to Perpetuity immutably the same." Similarly the number of the Board of Fellows was set at twelve with eight, including the president to be Baptists and "the rest indifferently of any or all Denominations."[92] In the denominational listings such as that of Morgan Edwards, the Seventh Day Baptists are listed among the Baptists indicating their acceptance with no discrimination for their Sabbath distinctive.[93]

---

[90] Walter C.,Bronson, *The History of Brown University 1764-1914* (Providence RI: Brown University 1914) p 7.

[91] *Historical Catalogue of Brown University 1764-1914* (Providence, RI: Brown University 1914) pp 22-26.

[92] "The Charter of Brown University" in *Historical Catalogue* pp.12-13.

[93] Eva Weeks and Mary Edwards, ed., Materials Towards *A History of the Baptists* by Morgan Edwards A.M. and fellow of Rhode Island College 1779-1792 (Danielsville, GA: Heritage Papers 1984) Vol. I p. 197.

Enoch and Ebenezer David: A Seventh Day Baptist, Ebenezer David, was a member of the fourth graduating class at Brown receiving his degree in 1772. His father, Enoch David, was a lay-preacher in the Philadelphia area, earning his living as a tailor during the week, but preaching among several Seventh Day Baptist churches on Saturdays. Occasionally he preached on Sunday in some of the more numerous congregations of First-Day Baptists in Philadelphia. He also made several evangelistic tours in Pennsylvania and New Jersey. Enoch David was sufficiently prosperous to send his son, Ebenezer, to the newly organized Baptist college in Rhode Island. The Providence Gazette in its coverage of the 1772 commencement at Rhode Island College reported: "After the degrees had been conferred, the valedictory oration was pronounced by Ebenezer David who took as a subject, *The Incomparable Advantages of Religion*."[94] During his college years Ebenezer attended the Seventh Day Baptist Church at Newport whenever possible. Deacon John Tanner apparently took a special interest in the young student and corresponded with his father. A letter written August 2, 1773 carries a note with Ebenezer's address saying, "To be left with Mr. John Tanner in Newport." Within the letter, Enoch wrote that he liked the letters from John Tanner very much, "they shew the Breathings of a plain Harted Honest Comfortable Christian. I seem as if I had seen the man and Conversed with him face to Face which is not true."[95]

Ebenezer David was baptized and joined the church at Newport in 1770. The church licensed him to preach in 1773. In 1775 the Newport Church called him to ordination so that he might have power to administer the ordinances of the gospel as an itinerant preacher as he returned to Philadelphia. An invitation from the church signed by John Tanner, William Bliss and Job Bennett was sent to the Hopkinton Church where the actual ordination took place. His letters tell of working his way through Connecticut, New York and New Jersey often preaching two or three times a day. In 1776 Ebenezer David was appointed chaplain to two regiments in the Continental Army, one from Rhode Island and the other from Massachusetts. He served with the army during the sieges of Boston, New York, and engagements at Ticonderoga, Peekskill, the Hudson Highlands and the defense of the Delaware. In December 1777 he was with the troops in encampment at Valley Forge. During part of this time he received furloughs

---

[94] Jeanette Black and William Greene Roelker, ed. *A Rhode Island Chaplain in the Revolution, Letters of Ebenezer David to Nicholas Brown 1775-1778* (Providence, RI: The Rhode Island Society of Cincinnati 1949) p. xviii.

[95] Original Manuscript letter to Enoch David to Ebenezer, August 2, 1773 in SDB Historical Society archives, Janesville, WI Ms 19x.470.

to study medicine with plans to transfer to the medical corps. On February 3, 1778 he was assigned to the hospital at Lancaster where he fell prey to "the putrid fever" and died March 19th.

From June of 1775 to February of 1778, Ebenezer carried on an extensive correspondence with Nicholas Brown, a successful Providence merchant and one of the incorporators of Rhode Island College. Many of those letters to Nicholas were preserved providing a primary source of information about life in the army and the strategy as viewed from within the ranks. Nicholas Brown's son, Nicholas, Jr. graduated from the college in 1786 and became such a benefactor of the college that in 1804 the name of the college was changed to Brown University.

Economic Leadership: John Tanner was a member of the Newport Seventh Day Baptist Church whose success in his profession made it possible to give leadership in other areas. John Tanner was born in 1712 of parents who were members of the Hopkinton Seventh Day Baptist Church. As a young man he moved to Newport where he became a successful goldsmith. He was baptized and became a member of the Newport Church in 1737 and soon thereafter was elected as trustee. He also served as clerk of the church for thirty-five years. In 1760 he was ordained a deacon and served with distinction until his death in 1785. Many of the business meetings of the church were held in his home.

He was one of the trustees of Rhode Island College who, according to Walter C. Bronson, made a significant contribution to the college with the gift of one hundred and thirty-five volumes of miscellaneous works especially valuable for the study of New England church history.[96] Tanner was greatly affected financially and socially by the Revolutionary War. When the British army occupied Newport, Deacon Tanner was persecuted because of he was a "zealous patriot." He escaped some of the dangers by moving to a more rural retreat at Hopkinton. In 1776 his wife died and her tombstone contains the reference to "the storms and dangers of an unnatural and cruel civil war." He worshipped with the church at Hopkinton, while located there but his heart was still in Newport. With the withdrawal of the British from the island, Tanner returned and continued his professional craft and his voluntary leadership in the church as it sought to overcome difficulties created by the war and a change in the pastorate. His sense of covenant is demonstrated in a letter to one of the members who wanted to join in communion with the Presbyterian church in Norwich.

We as a church of Christ cannot give you liberty to leave us until we know the reasons you may have for withdrawing your communion with us. You express your love and regard for the

---

[96] Bronson, *The History of Brown University* p. 110.

church; but it is an old and true saying, that actions speak louder than words. You did not manifest such affection when you were here last, for you did not deign to meet with us on God's holy Sabbath, to worship on his holy day...

I beg that you would remember that solemn vows to God are not to be trifled with! You professed to own us as a true church of Christ near fifteen years ago. I entreat you to consider seriously what it is you are now aiming at, whether it will be to the glory of God, or your own soul's good, to break covenant with the church of Christ, which you engaged and covenanted to walk with, and join yourself to a church so contrary in practice. Pray, consider these things, and may the good Lord direct you to that which is right in his sight.[97]

John Tanner's will executed in 1785 shows concern for the economic survival of the church particularly in the support of the pastor. In addition to a testimony of faith in its preamble, there are many provisions concerning his material goods. For example, he willed, "To the Sabbatarian Baptist Church in Newport, (whereof I am a member) for the use of the minister or elder the dwelling house and lot of land which I bought from Mr. John Barker in said Newport." To the same church he also left "a sum of sixty pounds to be let out at interest for the use of the minister, a silver flagon for use of communion "(unless I should give one in my life time)," He aso willed much of his religious library which he listed with the added note: "to be kept in good order for the use of the said minister or ministers of the church forever, and not to be lent; and my mind and will is, that the trustees of said church for the time being shall visit the minister at least once a year in order to view said books, and see that none are lost, and that they are kept in good order."

Mr. Tanner also remembered the "Sabbatarian Church of Baptists in Hopkinton," and in Piscataway, New Jersey with grants of sixty pounds and thirty pounds respectively "to be put out and kept at interest, the income divided between the present ministers and their successors forever." Rhode Island College was bequeathed, "my clock that has my name upon it, to stand in the college hall forever" and all my books that are not herein particularly given away, and the sum of one hundred pounds." Others gifts to various family members and friends were listed in considerable detail, including his mansion, his clothing, (including his best suit to his pastor), and his second best bed to the first of William Bliss' daughters to marry. Of historic significance was an item in which he willed to William Bliss, the pew that the

---

[97] John Tanner, "Letter to Sister in Norwich," **Seventh Day Baptist Memorial July 1854** (New York City: Seventh Day Baptists Publishing Society 1854) vol 3: 3 p. 107-108.

widow Sanford and the widow Hastic sit in. This documents the fact that at least some of the pews were owned by various individuals, a practice common in many churches of the time.

Also of significance is the item beginning with the words, "My will and pleasure is, that at my decease my negro man Scipio shall be set free." Tanner also enumerated numerous items to be given to Scipio such as his everyday clothes, of shirts, socks, shoes and boot. He showed an awareness of problems caused by liberated slaves, and thus included in his will the statement, "And my mind and will is, and I hereby order, that in case my said negro man Scipio shall become chargeable to the town of Newport, that my nephew, James Tanner, shall indemnify the said town from all such charges out of that part of my estate which I have given him in this my will."[98]

Cultural Contributions: When the Preservation Cooperative report referred to the interior of the Seventh Day Baptist Meeting House as "a symbol of the wealth, education and talent of the distinguished members," no name stands above that of Henry Collins, one of the two members responsible for the construction of the 1730 structure. At a Reunion of the Sons and Daughters of Newport in 1859, a report in the Providence Journal contained an article on the history of the Redwood Library in Newport with attention given to the founders of the Society for the Promotion of Knowledge and Virtue which planted the seed for the establishment of the library. Of Henry Collins it reported:

Henry Collins was a distinguished merchant of Newport -- distinguished not only for his success in mercantile affairs, but also for his learning, refined taste in literature and the fine arts, benevolence and devotion to a wife and general diffusion of knowledge. He was thirty-one years of age at the time that he associated with the above-named men, for the purpose of founding a Literary and Philosophical Society, actively engaged in business, and ready with heart and hand to prosper every good and noble work --- one of the strongest evidences of which was the gift of land on which the Library now stands....

There was another noble trait in the character of Mr. Collins, which should not go unnoticed. Deserving young man, struggling with the world, and anxious to acquire a liberal education, found in him a true friend, and many who, but for this timely assistance would have passed through life unnoticed, became prominent

---

[98] The will of John Tanner. The original is in posession of the SDB Historical Society at Janesville WI. A copy is included in the Seventh Day Baptist Memorial vol 3:3 July 1854 p. 111.

through their acquirements and an ornament to society. Every measure, calculate to promote the public good, he heartily endorsed, and the extension of Long Wharf, the building of the Brick Market, now the City Hall, and other public works, owed much of their success to his liberality and countenance.[99]

He collected a gallery of paintings to such an extent that Dr. Waterhouse referred to Henry Collins as "the Lorenzo de Medici of Rhode Island."[100] He hired some of the finest artists in the country to paint portraits of the leading men in the city, including such pastors as John Callender of the Baptist Church, Nathaniel Clap of the Congregational Church, Dean Berkeley associated with Trinity Episcopal Church, and Thomas Hiscox of the Seventh Day Baptist Church. Thomas Hiscox, the son of William Hiscox, the first pastor of the Newport Church, was the pastor of the church at Hopkinton and a close friend of Henry Collins. He often preached at Newport, and worked with Collins in various church ministries. The portrait of Thomas Hiscox eventually became a part of the Vanderbilt collection in their Newport home known as The Breakers.

Henry Collins was born March 25, 1699 the son of Arnold and Amy Collins both of whom were highly respected in the town. Arnold was a goldsmith by trade and attained considerable wealth. He was a trustee of the Seventh Day Baptist church although there is no record of his baptism or acceptance into the church. The 1706 deed for the meeting house lot on Barney Street was made out to Arnold Collins. Henry's mother appears on the 1692 membership list of the church. She was the granddaughter of Roger Williams, and was first married to Thomas Ward who died in 1689. Governor Richard Ward was thus a half-brother to Henry Collins, and although considerably older the two were close friends.

The Annals of the Redwood Library records. "That the surroundings of young Collins had much to do with the formation of his character, and the development of a taste for literature, is apparent; for the Wards were men of sterling character...Henry Collins was sent to England to perfect his studies, and was there trained for a mercantile career; to which he gave such attention as secured the means, on his return, to indulge a refined taste for literature and the arts."

Upon his return from England Collins was baptized and became a member of the Seventh Day Baptist Church in 1728. He, along with Jonathan Weeden, is perhaps best remembered for his role in the building of the meeting house, but he served in other ways as well. In 1732 he was

---

[99] from George C. Mason, Reunion of the Sons and Daughters of New Port, RI (Newport RI: Fred A Pratt & Co. 1859) p. 230-232.

[100] Edward Peterson, *History of Rhode Island and Newport* (New York: John S Taylor, 1853) p. 91.

appointed to accompany Joseph Maxson and Thomas Hiscox "to visit some friends at the eastward in answer to their request to Sabbath keepers in this colony," .[101] Unfortunately, some of Collins' liberality during years of prosperity coupled with economic losses created by the Admiralty Rule of 1756 led to financial ruin and bankruptcy. He lost his home to his creditors and spent his remaining years under the roof of Ebenezer Flagg whom he had befriended and with whom he had entered into business partnership. The date of his death is unknown, although there is a record that in March 1766 Mr. George Rome advertised to settle the affairs of Henry Collins, deceased.

It is ironic that Henry Collins' home on Washington Street which was acquired by George Rome was later confiscated by the State during the revolutionary period because of Rome's loyalist leanings. It was later occupied by the family of Gilbert Stuart, the famous artist who is best known for his portrait of George Washington.[102] Henry Collins never married, but his legacy to Newport is still evident in the old Seventh Day Baptist Meeting House, the Redwood Library, the Brick Market, and the level of culture and art that he helped foster.

Musical Contribution: Seventh Day Baptists were also significant in the introduction of hymns in public worship. When the Congregationalists and Baptists separated from the Church of England, they rejected the Book of Common Prayer and other prewritten or prepared materials, which included hymns and poetry. One Baptist writer in 1691 said, "Singing by a set stinted form is the invention of man, being of the same quality as, if not worse than, common stilted set-form prayers, or even infant sprinkling. It is artificial, and therefore alien to free motions of the Spirit of God. He also noted that "some cannot sing, not having tunable voices, and women ought anyhow to keep silence in the churches."[103]

Gladys Bolhouse, in her paper on "Old Churches in Newport" wrote that when the first Methodist church in Newport was built in 1806, it had what was considered the first steeple for a Methodist church in this country. The Bishop of that time is said to have commented bitterly, "A steeple... they'll be having a choir next." She then commented that there was no singing in the Baptist church until 1764 when the church minutes read:

---

[101] Minutes of the Newport Seventh Day Baptist Church 1692-1846 p. 184-185, Stillman handscript copy CRR19x.78 SDB Historical Society archives.

[102] Henry E. Turner, "Henry Collins" in the *Rhode Island Historical Magazine* vol 5 no. 2 Oct. 1884 p. 84

[103] Mr. Steed, cited by B. J. Gilman, The Evolution of the English Hymn (New York: Macmillan 1927) p. 178.

A motion was then made for introducing singing which was referred to consideration....We appointed three of the brethren to go to the brethren in general and see how their minds were concerning singing praise to God in the church.... These brethren reported that the brethren in general consented to allow liberty to those brethren that had a mind to sing praise to God to sing... also agreed that if any of the brethren find it burdensome for them to stay at time of singing that they have liberty to withdraw or go out.[104]

Seventh Day Baptists, however, from the very beginning in America used hymns in their worship. The Seventh Day Baptists were among the first Protestants in England to regularly use hymns in their worship. As early as 1657 Thomas Tillam wrote a hymn for use in a communion service, linking the Sabbath and communion.[105] Joseph Stennett in 1696 wrote that "though the Psalms were good for general worship, something peculiarly Christian was needed for the Lord's Supper." By 1709 he had compiled and published fifty hymns for communion and another twelve for the sacrament of Baptism.[106] A letter from Peter Chamberlain to Samuel Hubbard dated August 1677 laments the fact that some oppose the singing of hymns. That this was a problem in America is seen in a letter of Hubbard to an acquaintance in Providence in 1681, as he referred to a newcomer who opposed singing in public. "It has been for some time omitted, but I hope the church will recover itself...."[107]

The church did recover itself and Seventh Day Baptists have been a singing people. Whether they influenced other churches of the time to sing may never be known, but it undoubtedly had its effect as they shared in worship and fellowship.

---

[104] Mrs. Gladys Bolthouse, "Old Churches of Newport" duplicated copy from Newport Historical Society Library p. 3-4

[105] Thomas Tillam, The Seventh Day Sabbath Sought Out and Celebrated, (London, by the author 1657) Microfilm copy in SDB Historical Society library from original at Union Theological Seminary NY, BV 125 T5 c 5 between pages 112 and 113.

[106] Joseph Stennett, "Hymns in commemoration of the Suffering of our Blessed Saviour, Jesus Christ, Composed for the Celebration of His Holy Supper," in The Works of the Late Reverend and Learned Mr. Joseph Stennett (London :1732) Vol. IV p. 49.

[107] *Hubbard's Journal* pp. 99, 121.

Chapter 6

PASTORAL MINISTRY

Six different men have been pastors of the Newport Seventh Day Baptist Church during its two hundred years of existence: William Hiscox (1671 -1704); William Gibson (1704 - 1718); Joseph Crandall (1718-1737) John Maxson (1754-1778). William Bliss (1778-1808) and Henry Burdick (180-1843). Several others gave interim service between pastorates or assisted in the carrying out of pastoral duties. Among the more prominent of these were: Joseph Maxson and Thomas Hiscox pastors at Hopkinton who provided service, particularly for the administration of the sacraments of baptism and communion during the years 1737-1754; Arnold Bliss of New Bedford, Massachusetts, who served during his father's declining years; and Lucius Crandall who was appointed by other churches as an evangelist or missionary pastor in an effort to revive the church.

Few had college or seminary education but that did not mean that they were ignorant or untrained. The list of books in their libraries indicated a knowledge of Latin, Greek and Hebrew, as well as many of the classics of theology. Most were trained in practical theology through experience or on the job training. That which Henry Clarke wrote in 1811 of William Bliss could be said of most of those early pastors. "He was a man of solid piety, judgement and information. He had a large library and useful books, and made good use of reading, while he much esteemed the soul-reviving influence of the spirit, when corresponding with the written Word."[108] All but William Gibson were called from within the ranks of the Newport or Hopkinton churches. Most were first called to the diaconate to assist the pastor, and then when the need arose, were called to pastoral ordination and remained in that church for life. Among Seventh Day Baptists of the time, the term *Elder* was generally used within the churches, however the term *Reverend* was often used in their relation to other churches and the community at large. Most Baptist pastors of the time were bi-vocational for they earned much of their support in farming or other occupations. In part this was of necessity, for their families were often quite large and resources were limited. Yet even where there was a measure of affluence, there was a reluctance on the part of many Baptists to have a paid clergy.

---

[108]   Henry Clarke, *A History of the Sabbatarians or Seventh Day Baptists in America Containing their Rise and Progress to the Year 1811 with their Leaders Names and their Distinguishing Tenets* (Utica, NY by the author 1811) p. 22.

William Hiscox, the first pastor, was one of the seven charter members of the church. Thomas B. Stillman describes the conditions which he faced as pastor in these words:

> Rhode Island was but a wilderness when he commenced his ministry, there being scarcely three hundred families in the colony; yet numbers of families in different parts of the colony were counted as members of his congregation, and nearly the whole settlement of Westerly had embraced the seventh day. There were living at the period of his death about one hundred members of the church, notwithstanding a period of great mortality had previously prevailed in the colony, and the drain of its young men during the destructive Indian Wars under King Philip, tended to reduce the number that may have been enrolled upon the church books. The loss of the records of the church for the first twenty-one years of its existence leaves us to conjecture as to the greater number during that period.[109]

As the sole Sabbatarian pastor in America, William Hiscox's parish extended beyond Newport and Hopkinton, then called Westerly. In 1674 he was sent to New London, Connecticut to work with the family of James Rogers. Although they observed the seventh day Sabbath, they held certain other beliefs which led them to form their own sect under the name of Rogerene Baptists. In 1703 Hiscox was sent to Pennsylvania to attempt to resolve differences within the group in that location. He died on May 24, 1704 at the age of 66 having served as pastor for thirty-three years.

William Gibson was the second pastor and the only one who did not come to the ministry from within. He was a member of the Bell Lane Seventh Day Baptist Church in England. His signature is attached to a letter of encouragement from that church to the Newport Sabbath keepers in 1668, three years before their separation from the First Baptists Church. The circumstances of his coming to Newport are unclear, for the church records for this period are missing. He and his wife accompanied Stephen Mumford on his return trip from England in 1675, leading some to believe that the Mumfords recruited him. On the other hand, a letter of recommendation from the Bell Lane Church recorded by Samuel Hubbard suggests that the Bell Lane Church or Gibson himself may have taken the initiative. The church commended the Gibsons and requested that he be permitted to "perform

---

[109] Thomas B. Stillman, ed. "William Hiscox" in *Seventh Day Baptist Memorial* (Seventh Day Baptist Publishing Society, NY: 1852) Vol. 1:1 p. 3-4.

duties and enjoy gospel privileges with you, his church and people," indicating that he probably had been ordained in England and had been in full communion for several years.110

Gibson settled in Newport, but soon moved to a farm near Hopkinton. Together with Elder John Crandall and Elder John Maxson, he began to relieve William Hiscox of some of the ministerial duties in the scattered parish. At the death of William Hiscox, in 1704, Gibson was called to the pastorate. One of his early duties as pastor was a response to the request of the Piscataway, New Jersey Seventh Day Baptist church to ordain their pastor, Edmund Dunham. This service was held at Hopkinton October 11, 1705.

During Gibson's pastorate the members living in the Westerly or Hopkinton area separated from the Newport Church to become a separate congregation. Many of the church meetings had alternated between the two locations, but at a meeting in Hopkinton in 1708, it was voted that "that part of the congregation in and about Westerly shall be henceforth a distinct congregation by themselves, and also that part of the congregation in and about Rhode Island shall be a distinct Church from that at Westerly, provided the brethren and sisters in Newport that are not present at said meeting concur thereunto."[111] There may have been some reluctance on the part of the Newport congregation for there were only forty-one members at Newport while Hopkinton numbered seventy-two. Nonetheless they answered, "If Brother Joseph Crandall may at the least for the present perform the administration of baptism to both them and us, they can and do consent." Thus began the apprenticeship of the third pastor, Joseph Crandall, who assumed more of the responsibility of the Newport Church even though William Gibson remained the official pastor till his death in 1717.

Joseph Crandall, the third pastor, was the son of Elder John Crandall who had been prominent in the Baptist Church of John Clarke and represented Baptists in their struggles with the established churches in Massachusetts and Connecticut. Joseph had married Deborah Burdick, the daughter of Robert and Ruth Hubbard Burdick, the granddaughter of Samuel and Tacy Hubbard. Their names appear on the 1692 roll of the Newport Church.

Even before his ordination to the diaconate in 1709, he had been chosen to represent the church on several occasions. In 1703 he accompanied William Hiscox on his mission to smooth difficulties among the churches in Pennsylvania. In 1715 he was called to ordination as an elder by the Newport

---

110 *Hubbard's Journal,* p. 82.

111 Minutes of the yearly meeting at the Church at Westerly the 17th of the 7th month 1708

Church and two years later assumed the pastorate upon the death of William Gibson. The Meeting House was built during the pastorate of Joseph Crandall. Of this period Thomas B. Stillman noted that "the society of Newport was generally well informed; but during his administration there was a constellation of intelligent and literary characters there, never before equaled in New England. Among them were John Callender, Dean Berkeley, Richard Ward, Henry Collins and Thomas Ward, some of them members of his congregation..." He had not the learning of his venerable predecessor, but was a sound and faithful preacher of the gospel; strict in his discipline, yet courteous of all.[112]

Of the discipline which he administered, C. H. Greene wrote, " The church records are saturated with cases of discipline, admonition and council; church meetings being of very frequent occurrence. The soul of a member was deemed of such precious worth, that the church could not let them go without a struggle. There were few cases where the erring one was not finally reclaimed. Some cases were allowed to run on for three or four years before they were finally settled and the brother or sister being reconciled to the church."[113] Elder Crandall died in September of 1737 and the church was without an official pastor for seventeen years. During this interim Thomas Hiscox and Joseph Maxson from the Hopkinton church assisted the members of the Newport congregation in maintaining services and administering the sacraments. Thomas Hiscox, the fourth pastor at Hopkinton, was the son of Elder William Hiscox, the first pastor. Joseph Maxson, on the other hand was the son of John Maxson Sr. the first pastor of the Hopkinton congregation. Joseph's wife was Tacy Burdick, a sister of Joseph Crandall's wife and a granddaughter of Samuel and Tacy Hubbard. The Hopkinton church had specifically ordained these two as evangelists or traveling ministers "empowered to administer the ordinances of the gospel as they may be occasionally called by either of the churches."[114]

John Maxson, the fourth pastor, was the grandson of John Maxson Sr. the first pastor of the Westerly or Hopkinton church. He was the nephew of both the second and the fourth pastors at Westerly, and his sister had married the son of Thomas Hiscox, the third pastor. Both his father and mother were grandchildren of Samuel and Tacy Hubbard. It is little wonder that so many of the current Seventh Day Baptist families claim descent from charter members of the Newport Church.

---

[112] Stillman, "Joseph Crandall" *Seventh Day Baptist Memorial*, vol. no. 1 January 1852, p. 8

[113] Charles H. Greene, manuscript , N*ew Port Rhode Island* p. 34

[114] Church minutes of the Newport and Hopkinton Church, October 8, 1732.

John Maxson was called to exercise his gifts by the church in Westerly in 1843 at age 30 and submitted to an examination before the church. For some reason he declined the call at that time, but in 1750 he was chosen as a deacon with authority to administer the sacrament of baptism and preach. Four years later he was called to ordination as an elder and on November 24, 1754 he became the pastor. His pastorate from 1754 to 1778 was during one of the most crucial periods in American history. It began with the start of the French and Indian War in which the French lost Canada and much of the American Midwest. It was a time when the British tightened control on the American colonies, in part to pay for the expense of the war. His pastorate ended in the midst of the Revolutionary War when the outcome was in considerable doubt. His sons served in the Continental Army along with other young men of his parish. Much of his congregation was scattered and those who were engaged in shipping and trade suffered many losses.

But it was also a period of considerable influence for the future. Among the sixty-one members added to the church during John Maxson's pastorate were: Governor Richard Ward; Judge Henry Bliss; Senator Joseph Carpenter; Joseph Southwick (great grandfather of James Southwick, the chairman of the Newport Historical Society Improvement Committee which recommended the purchase of the Meeting House in 1884); William Bliss, Maxson's successor as pastor; Chaplain Ebenezer David; and Col. Job Bennett, trustee and treasurer of Brown University. Elder Maxson himself was a trustee of Brown University for fourteen years, from the beginning of the college in 1764 until his death in 1778.

His most important ministry, however, was not to the famous but to the common people of Newport. Prior to the Revolutionary War Newport had a population of 12,000 and commerce was second to none. In 1775 the British fleet entered the harbor and the town was occupied by an estimated 8,000 troops of King George III. During that period Newport was under martial law, nearly 500 buildings were destroyed, and most of the trees and burnable shrubs were used for fuel. When the British left, the wells were filled up, many wharves were destroyed and much other wanton damage was done by order of the British commander. All but two churches were used as barracks or riding stables thus most public worship was suspended. But Elder Maxson went from house to house throughout the city encouraging all, regardless of their church affiliation, to stand firm and trust in God. Many credit him with preserving the nucleus of several churches which came to life again after the occupation ended.

The Maxson name was attached to one of the oldest houses in Newport which was located near the first Seventh Day Baptist meeting house. Some traditions claimed this house was occupied by three Maxson pastors of the church, even though only one was ever pastor there. (The other two were pastors in Westerly or Hopkinton.) The church records mention the gift of a house, for the benefit of the pastor, but imply that the rental was to go to their support. The records do not give the location for that house, although there are references to a house on a hill which came from the Ward family. In 1944 the "Maxson House" as it came to be known, was sold to a merchant who wanted to construct a commercial building on its location. Efforts were made to have the building moved and thus preserved as the parsonage of the Seventh Day Baptist Church. The Newport Historical Society was hesitant in moving the building to their lot, so the Georgian Society of Rhode Island undertook to preserve the historic house, and asked for support from the Seventh Day Baptist Historical Society.[115] A thorough search of the records including deeds and wills failed to substantiate the tradition that the "Maxson House" was ever the property of the church, or that John Maxson and his family ever lived in it.[116] The March 13, 1945 issue of *The Sun* published in Westerly R. I. reported that when no definite proof could be found that the Maxson house was the parsonage, the Seventh Day Baptist Historical Society dropped its effort at preservation. This lack of proof plus the poor condition of the house likewise caused the Newport Historical Society to decline any participation in its preservation.[117]

Thus in 1945 a building which may have stood the ravages of time and which might have been architecturally significant because of its age fell to the demolition crew. To the historian, a tradition based upon improper assumptions without proper documentation has little historical value. Although the "Maxson House" is gone, the "house of Maxson" lives on, not in buildings but in the memory of a distinguished family whose contributions extend to the present. His tomb stone in the old burying ground near the Perry monument, bears the fitting inscription:

In memory of Elder John Maxson, Pastor of ye Sabbatarian Baptist Church in Newport, who departed this life March 2nd, A. D. 1778, in the 65th year of his age, justly esteemed for his Christian virtues and exemplary life.[118]

---

[115] Correspondence between William King Covell of the Georgian Society and Corliss F. Randolph *et. al.* of the SDB Historiacal Society December 1944 -- April 1945.

[116] Letter from Mrs. Susan Bradley Franklin to the SDB Historical Socciety, February 1945.

[117] *The Sun* Westerly, R. I. Tuesday March 13, 1945.

[118] Taken from the tombstone in the old burying ground at Newport, Sept. 1993.

William Bliss became the fifth pastor of the Newport church. He was born in 1728, the son of Josiah Bliss, and either a grandson or a great grandson of Governor Benedict Arnold.[119] In his younger years he "cast off the restraints of parental education to join with irreligious young men in skeptical debates," and openly professed himself a Deist.[120] He accepted a captain's commission in the colonial army and was on the point of marching with troops raised for an expedition against the French in Canada when a treaty led to peace between England and France and the troops were disbanded in 1763.

Bliss married Barbara Phillips in 1750 but it was fourteen years later that the two were baptized and joined the church. To that union seven sons and five daughters were born, several of whom were to play significant rolls in his life and that of the church. In a poem which William Bliss wrote for his children, possibly at the time of the death of one of his daughters, he expressed the change which took place in his life.

> At thirty-five, I serious grew,
> And had another world in view---
> Thought oft about a future state,
> And what was like to be my fate.
>
> I thought of death, and that great day
> When heaven and earth must pass away;
> Then asked my soul, "Come answer true,
> How stands the case 'tween God and you.

After describing some of his consciousness of personal guilt and questionings he concluded:

> One day, as sitting by the fire,
> My soul was filled with strong desire;
> I thought of what the Scripture said
> Of Christ and the atonement made.
>
> How beautiful the gospel seemed.
> When God was honored, man redeemed!
> I thought that God forgave my sin;

---

[119] Governor Arnold's will dated 1677 gives his daughter, Damaris Bliss "a parcel of land in the precinct of Newport." Some records indicate that Damaris was married to John Bliss, Josiah's father, while others show Damaris as Josiah's wife. Her name appears on the church roll of the Newport churh in 1708 while Josiah's appears following baptism in 1712.

[120] "William Bliss " in Seventhn Day Baptist Memorial, vol.1 p.14.

I found myself at peace within.[121]

The church recognized the potential for leadership in William Bliss and in 1773 voted that William Bliss exercise his gift in public, by preaching the gospel and issued a license "to preach publicly among us or elsewhere when called thereunto."[122] After the death of Elder John Maxson, William Bliss was ordained to the work of the evangelical ministry at the church in Hopkinton in 1779. A year later he was officially installed as pastor of the Newport church, a position he held for twenty-eight years.

Those years embraced the continued occupation of British troops in Newport, the concluding of peace, a changed economy on the island and the ever increasing migration from Newport to the west. With the establishment of new churches there was the felt need to expand the Yearly Meetings to include other churches for fellowship and missionary outreach. Newport was one of the eight churches which formed the Seventh Day Baptist General Conference in 1802.[123] The years between his being licensed to preach and his installation as pastor were particularly hard for William Bliss. His wife died in 1775 at age forty-eight. leaving him with a large family, the youngest but five years of age. The British soldiers which were quartered on his farm caused considerable damage as they cut down his orchard, burned his fences and plundered his cattle and crops. It is reported that some of the soldiers accompanied Bliss as he hunted along the coast. When they marveled at his marksmanship, he is said to have remarked, "You seem to be very anxious for the Americans to land upon the island. Now when they come, they will take you down as easy as I do these birds."[124]

His daughters showed their sentiments toward the British in slightly different fashion. One day while the officers were away, Elizabeth and Barbary climbed the embankment where the British flag had been raised, lowered the flag, tore it into thirteen strips and hoisted it back up the pole. Upon the return of the officers, a reward was offered for the perpetrators of the offense, but the girls were never suspected. Their younger sister, Mary, showed her contempt by taking one of the officer's finest sword, thrust it through a hole in the plastering and let it drop between the studding. It remained there until after the war, when it was taken out as a trophy of female valor.[125]

---

[121] *SDB Memorial* v. 1 p. 15

[122] Church minutes, September 19, 1773.

[123] The constituting churches were: Newport and Hopkinton in Rhode Island, Waterford and Burlingon in Connecticut, Petersburg (Berlin) and First Brookfield in New York, and Piscataway and Cohansie (Shilloh) in New Jersey.

[124] SDB Memorial, footnote p. 17.

[125] Footnote to "Arnold Bliss" in SDB Memorial V. 3 pp. 57-58.

Just prior to William Bliss' call to serve as pastor he remarried, taking as his wife Elizabeth Ward, the youngest daughter of Governor Richard Ward and sister of Gov. Samuel Ward. Together they earned a reputation for effective ministry. Elizabeth's hand is seen in an article in the *Newport Herald* of 1789 which reported that "a number of the good women of three different societies, viz., of the Sabbatarian Baptists, the first Day Baptist and the first Congregational Church in Newport, met at the house of Elder Bliss in Middletown.... The afternoon was spent in harmony, in freedom of conversation on religious subjects and singing the praise of God; and after refreshing themselves, the elder gave a lecture suited to the occasion, from Exodus 35:25." This passage referred to "all the women that were wise-hearted."[126]

Ninety five members were added to the church during his pastorate, twenty of whom carried the name Bliss, either as children, daughters-in-law or grandchildren. At least one son, Arnold, and one grandson, William Bliss Maxson entered the Seventh Day Baptist ministry. As an evangelist, Bliss helped to quicken the faith in the Hopkinton Church and on at least one occasion in 1789 was engaged with the Shrewesbury Seventh Day Baptist Church in New Jersey just prior to its move to western Virginia. In 1821 when the Seventh Day Baptist General Conference printed its first hymn book at least eight hymns written by Elder Bliss were included. Elder Bliss' ministry extended beyond his local parish for he was often in demand to fill the pulpit of other churches in Newport. He served on the Board of Trustees at Brown University from 1785 to 1793. In 1791 he was elected as an honorary member of the Redwood Library Company.

In 1808 he approached his death with a great testimony to the faith he had lived. The day before his death his grandson, William Bliss Maxson had returned from a long sea voyage. Elder Bliss interrupted his conversation saying that he no longer wanted to talk of earthly things for he was going to leave this world for what he believed to be a better one. The pastor of one of the other Baptists churches in town, Rev. Eddy visited him that same day and Bliss asked him to preach his funeral sermon saying, "I am going to try the truth of my doctrine." By the next morning Elder William Bliss made good on his resolve. His body was buried in a family plot in Middletown, but the grave stone has since been moved so that in 1993 it could be found leaning against the foundation of the Newport Historical Society.

Henry Burdick was the sixth and last pastor of the Newport Seventh Day Baptist Church. He was the son of Captain Icabod Burdick and Bathsheba Mackee Burdick. Through his grandfather, Robert Burdick 3rd,

---

[126] *Newport Herald*, April 23, 1789, reprinted in the *Sabbath Recorder*, March 22, 1926, v. 100 p. 353

and his grandmother, Susannah Clarke, he was the great, great, grandson of both Ruth and Bethiah Hubbard, daughters of Samuel and Tacy Hubbard. He was born in Westerly in 1767 and was baptized and joined the church at Newport in 1802. In January 1807 it was unanimously voted that "Brother Henry Burdick be requested to improve his gift in preaching the gospel to us, as often as opportunity offers and he has freedom." In November the church voted that he "receive ordination as Evangelist and be clothed with the authority of a gospel minister." The following month he was ordained and upon the death of Elder William Bliss, he assumed the role of pastor, a position he held until his death in 1843, a period of 35 years.

Henry Clarke who personally knew Elder Burdick spoke of him as "a pius, promising young man,"[127] and others spoke of his particular gift of prayer and great piety and earnestness. However, there is evidence that personal relations were not his strong suite. C. H. Greene wrote of him:

> Rev. Henry Burdick was a man of Puritanic mold of mind; having marked out for himself the exact line of truth and duty, he required of all his flock to march in the same straight and narrow way that his own feet trod. There could not be two views of Truth to him. Truth was one and indivisible. Therefore he knew not how to "stoop to conquer," nor yet how to persuade the erring in love and tenderness --- he must rebuke and drive.

It so came to pass that in his pastorate many of the heads of the families of his church were seafaring men, men who had all the sailors virtues and some of their faults. When these by the very nature of their calling, had never been baptized, but naturally thought of themselves as Seventh Day Baptists, and would, doubtless, have sometime been brought into the church ---. these men, when on shore, went to meeting in the morning and then went where they pleased. The next time they came to church, Elder Burdick would sternly rebuke them for "Sabbath Breaking." After a few such experiences they ceased to come at all and went where they were more welcome. This failing of the Rev. Henry Burdick was called among his colleagues "his scattering gift."[128] During his long pastorate, twenty-six people were added, ten males and sixteen women. Most were members of either the Bliss family or the Burdick family. The last trustee of the church, John Congdon was grandson of Elder Henry Burdick.

Although the church passed out of existence shortly after his pastorate ended, there were many circumstances which were beyond his control. As Lucius Crandall wrote for Burdick's obituary, "He was a man of sound and

---

[127] Henry Clarke, *A History of the Sabbatarian or Seventh Day Baptists,* p. 22

[128] C. H. Greene, typescript paper, New Port," Rhode Island," pp 51-52

exalted piety, His humble and uniform confidence in God -- his habitual deep solicitude for the prevalence of pure religion -- the revival of the church here -- and the peculiar and deep devotion and strong intercession which characterized his prayers, afford a firm and pleasing foundation for high and rich hopes on his behalf and comfort to the numerous family and friends which he has left to mourn, though not without hope."[129]

[129] Lucius Crandall, "Obituary for Henry Burdick," The Seventh Day Baptist Register, Vol. 4 :34, October 18, 1843 p. 135.

Chapter 7

GONE BUT NOT FORGOTTEN

At the beginning of the twentieth century William L. Burdick summarized the fate of the Newport Seventh Day Baptist Church with these words:

> Different ones might give different reasons for its decline, but two things are evident: (1) the tide of emigration was away from it because there were better opportunities westward; and (2) the society in Newport was not one which would seriously consider an unpopular truth. The history of the church was one of internal peace and quiet, seldom rent with dissensions within. During its two hundred years, it sent out very many to witness to the truth elsewhere, the light radiated from it far and near, but a fashionable summer resort is not a place where we would naturally expect a church heralding unpopular truth to flourish.[130]

L. E. Livermore, writing in 1892, expressed a slightly different diagnosis when he wrote:

> The old mother church at Newport, Rhode Island founded in 1671 should have been nursed back into life and vigor instead of passing out of our hands to be preserved as a historic fossil. It did not necessarily die of old age. Christianity is not old. It is not feeble. Churches should be perpetuated from age to age, century to century, growing stronger and more efficient as the years go by. Newport should be one of our living churches today.[131]

Expressed in these two statements are several basic diagnoses for the decline and eventual closing of the Newport Seventh Day Baptist Church. Livermore suggested that the denomination or the association should have "nursed" the church back to life. Attempts were made by the Missionary Board to try to give "artificial resuscitation" to the church. They appointed a

---

[130] William L. Burdick, "Eastern Association" from *Seventh Day Baptists in Europe and America,* (Plainfield NJ: American Sabbath Tract Society 1910) Vol. 2: no. 3 p. 131.

[131] L. E. Livermore, "Home Mission Word of the Eastern Association" in *Jubilee Papers* (Westerly, RI: Seventh Day Baptist Missionary Society 1892) p. 29-30.

missionary pastor, Lucius Crandall, to renew interest in Newport, but the effort met with little success. When a church has served its purpose or lost its sense of mission, an infusion of life from outside can only give temporary relief and postpone the inevitable. It was true, as William L. Burdick stated, the society of Newport had changed and the church could not appeal or reach the needs of a "fashionable resort."

The pastorate of Henry Burdick was marked by a puritanical legalism which appeared to place a prescribed code of conduct ahead of a personal relation to Christ. The minutes of the church from 1813 to 1836 reveal that although twenty-one were baptized (mostly children of members) there were sixteen who were dismissed for failure to abide by the covenant relations deemed necessary. Among these were Jeremiah Bliss and his wife, Mary. Jeremiah. the son of Elder William Bliss, was ordained a deacon in 1811 and was later appointed a trustee. He served capably for a number of years but in 1816 he was brought before the church for what was considered "a want of strictness in keeping the Sabbath." Not mentioned in the minutes but intimated from other sources was that "his connection with the Masonic Order operated unfavorably in respect to reconciliation."[132] After several years of meetings, the church voted to write a letter of "dismission or exclusion from the fellowship of the church for Jeremiah Bliss and his wife."[133] A footnote in the *Seventh Day Baptist Memorial* of April 1854 states that his connection with the custom-house, and other things "operating unfavorably upon his religious duties," caused him to be lost to the denomination, and the church of his early love."[134] It may be open to question whether a more understanding approach should have been taken, but the loss of such a leader was felt deeply by the church.

The church at Newport relied more heavily on "biological growth" than evangelism. Of the 120 members added to the church during the pastorates of William Bliss and Henry Burdick sixty-six carried the name of Bliss, Maxson, Burdick, Clarke or Crandall, all descendants of Samuel and Tacy Hubbard. Many of the others were also related to long established members. Much of the effort of the church was spent in trying to reclaim the members of the family rather than reaching out to others. In a family oriented church, it is easy to appear exclusive making it difficult for new members to feel kinship within a predominately church family.

The experience of Arnold Bliss, a son of Elder William Bliss, illustrates another possible cause of decline. He was ordained as an evangelist and worked with a branch of the Newport church at Ponegansett, near New Bedford, Massachusetts. A review of his ministry notes that a branch was

---

132 *Seventh Day Baptist Memorial* vol. 2: p. 94.
133 Church minutes for May 7, 1825.
134 *Seventh Day Baptist Memorial* vol. 3: p. 58.

authorized "for the purpose of accommodating the members residing there with the privilege of the gospel ordinances at home, yet without the responsibility of a church organization to stimulate them to the kind of labor which generally results in the firm and enduring continuance of church interest."[135]

Although these internal situations may have contributed to the dissolution of the Newport church, the greatest cause was, as William Burdick suggested, the tide of emigration away from it because there were better opportunities westward. From its very beginning, two of the Hubbard's three daughters had moved to Misquamicut, or the area known as Westerly. Samuel Hubbard reported that in 1678 there were twenty members in Newport, ten in New London and seven in Westerly. By 1708 when the Westerly or Hopkinton church was constituted as a separate church, seventy-two of the members lived in Westerly and only forty-one were left in Newport. During the next century the membership in Newport increased to about ninety while that of Hopkinton reached over eight hundred, many of whom formed the nucleus of other churches in Connecticut, New York, New Jersey and points west.

Often overlooked in this migration is the impact of the War of 1812 on a community such as Newport. The minutes of the Newport church in 1813 lists nine members, Daniel Burdick, Augustus and Jedediah Clarke, Polly Burdick, William, Jonathan, and John Maxson, Sally Stillman and Susanna Bliss, "removed from hence in time of war" and coming under the care of the sister church at Hopkinton.[136] This war had several effects upon Newport and its members. Two of the principal causes of the war were the impressment of American sailors and the disruption of sea trade. Mrs. Mary Bliss (Maxson) Greenman who died in Milton, Wisconsin in 1892 at the age of eighty-four recalled that when she was only five years old, she gathered some smaller children in the hospital under her father's care at Newport, and took them into a cellar of the building out of danger when she heard the booming of the cannon of the British ships threatening an attack upon the town in the last war with England.[137]

The War of 1812 also opened up much of the frontier for settlements. Trails were blazed and roads were built through the Appalachians. Many

---

[135] *Seventh Day Baptist Memorial* vol. 3: p. 58. "Arnold Bliss cultivated a farm in Ponegansett which had been a part of a tract owned by Gov. Richard Ward. He had willed the land to his daughter, Elizabeth who in turn sold it to her husband, Elder William Bliss, for the sum of $1 that it might be given to Arnold as a parental token." p. 54.

[136] Church minutes for August 27, 1813.

[137] "Mary Bliss Greenman," *The Sabbath Recorder* vol. 48:22, June 2, 1892 p. 341.

veterans were given land grants for their services and the Indian threat was largely removed through treaties. Some of the migrations were single one step moves from Rhode Island to the western frontier, others were made in three or four stages. In a small rural town in western New York, in a cemetery which was colloquially called "Little Rhode Island" there is a tall memorial bearing the name Bliss. On two of its sides are the epitaphs of Ebenezer and Martha Bliss and their two children, Eliza and David, all born in Newport R. I.. The third side has the inscription: "Wm. B. Bliss, A Union Color Bearer Died near Richmond, VA, June 28, 1862, Aged 24 yr. 3 mos. 2 da." Ebenezer was born 1796 the son of Thomas Ward Bliss and the grandson of Elder William Bliss. Both Ebenezer and Martha joined the Newport church in 1823, but were listed in 1827 as constituent members of the Little Genesee Seventh Day Baptist Church in Allegany County, New York. On that same list of members were Joel Crandall, Hulda (Maxson) Crandall, Henry C. Crandall, Amos Greene, Mary Maxson and Clarissa Tanner all from Rhode Island churches.[138]

The Greenman family represents a multi-stage migration pattern. The immigrant, John Greenman, came to Massachusetts in 1631 but soon moved to Rhode Island where he was admitted as a freeman in 1638. He joined the Baptist Church of John Clarke in 1644. His son, Edward became a freeman in Newport in 1655, but moved to Westerly in 1661. Two of his sons, Edward, Jr. and Thomas, were charter members of the Hopkinton Church. From Edward's family came the ship building family of Mystic, Connecticut. The Greenmansville Seventh Day Baptist Church founded in 1850 provided Sabbath worship for many of the workers who shared their belief. Their church building was moved to the grounds of the Mystic Seaport Museum and is now known as the Aloha Assembly Hall.

Thomas Greenman's son, Sylvanus, joined the Newport church in 1759. About 1776 Sylvanus, Jr. his mother and a brother, William, moved to Stephentown, New York were they became early members of the Petersburg (now Berlin) church in 1780. William Greenman's son, Reynolds, represents the next stage in the migration as he was one of the founders of the Brookfield Church in Central New York in 1797. The seventh generation included Reynold's son, Henry Giles Greenman. His mother was the daughter

---

[138] Joel Crandall was a fifth generation from Rev. Joseph Crandall and a sixth generation from both Ruth and Rachel Hubbard. Hulda Maxson Crandall was a fifth generation from Elder John Maxson and a sixth generation from Bethiah Hubbard. Joel and Hulda's daughter, Julia, married Benjamin F. Burdick also a descendant of Ruth Hubbard. This Julia and Benjamin Burdick are the great grandparents of the author of this history who grew up in the membership of the Little Genesee, NY church.

70

of Elder Henry Clarke who is often considered the founder of the General Conference and who wrote the first history of the denomination in 1811. In 1834 Henry and his family moved to Alfred in Allegany County where he became financial agent for Alfred University. He also acted as chorister for the Second Alfred Seventh Day Baptist Church until the family moved to Milton, Wisconsin in 1851. He opened a lumber yard there and served in a number of civic positions including the Board of Trustees for Milton College.[139]

Henry Greenman's wife in her own life time encompassed each of the moves of her husband's family. Mary Bliss (Maxson) Greenman was a granddaughter on her father's side of Elder John Maxson the fourth pastor of the Newport Church. Her mother, Mary Bliss was a cousin of Rev. William Bliss. She was seven years old when she left Newport to live with a half-brother at Stephentown. In her later years she recalled not only her taking children to the basement during the War of 1812 but attending service in the old Meeting House with its square box pews and high pulpit. She was also influenced by the nostalgic stories told of such members of the church as the Wards, Henry Collins, John Tanner and her own ancestors, the Hubbards. When she became of age she moved to Brookfield to help take care of her half-brother, Elder William Bliss Maxson.[140] Here she met and married Henry Greenman, while her sister, Tacy, married Datus Lewis. Datus and Tacy's son, Abram H. Lewis, became the most prolific writer and preacher for the Sabbath in denominational history.

These glimpses of the emigration from the mother church at Newport can be repeated many fold in the migrations to Shrewsbury, New Jersey, a church which later migrated as a body to West Virginia with further migrations of some of the same families into Ohio, Iowa, Nebraska and to the Pacific. The soul and spirit of the Newport Sabbatarian Church lives on in the lives of countless men and women who trace their spiritual lineage back to those who founded the church in 1671 and are reminded of its foundations by the carefully preserved Meeting House built in 1730, and so well preserved by the Newport Historical Society.

A modern hymn by Christian Ostergaard expresses reflections on the history of the Newport church "That cause can neither be lost nor stayed

---

[139] Peter Holden Greenman, The Greenman Family in America (Cohasset, MA: Greenman Family Assoc., 1988) p. 50-55

[140] William Bliss Maxson was the grandson of both Pastors John Crandall and William Bliss. He was a seaman in his early life, but later accepted the call to the ministry and was editor of the *Missionary Magazine,* edited *A Hymn Book for Seventh Day Baptist Churches*, served in several editorial capacities with *The Sabbath Recorder*.

Which takes the course of what God has made." Then in making comparison of a cause to the growth of a tree with branches stretching out as far as its roots go deep, the author concludes: "Be then no more by a storm dismayed, For by it the full-grown seeds are laid. And though the tree by its might it shatters, What then, if thousands of seeds it scatters!"

The Newport Seventh Day Baptist Church was not able to weather the storms that shook it, but it scattered the seeds further than any could have imagined over three hundred years ago.

PART TWO
MEMBERSHIP RECORDS

The recognized beginning of Baptists in America was in the Providence Plantations which later became Rhode Island. Roger Williams purchased land from the Indians in 1636 and three years later established a church of "rebaptized" members upon profession of faith, a basic principle in Baptist theology. The second major settlement in Rhode Island was on the island of Aquidneck which later took the name of Newport. Under the leadership of Dr. John Clarke a second Baptist Church was founded in 1644 which drew dissenters from neighboring Puritan colonies as well as from England. It was from this First Baptist Church of Newport that several other churches emerged, including the first Seventh Day Baptist Church in America founded in 1671. The events leading to the division were recorded in considerable detail in the First Baptist Church records, whereas the records of the Seventh Day Baptist Church from its inception to the year 1692 were lost. It may also be noted that a prior separation took place in 1656 when about twenty members withdrew over interpretation of the six principles records in the 6th chapter of Hebrews. (The names of the "Six Principle Baptist Church" constitute numbers 13-32 in the first list below.)

Thus the first few pages of the Newport Baptist Church records contain the names of members who withdrew in 1671 as well as others who were later listed in the 1692 records. At the tiem of the separation a number of those embracing the seventh day Sabbath, including part of the Hubbard family were widely scattered in that part of Rhode Island which was called Westerly and later Hopkinton.

A. Newport First Baptist Church 1644-1708
Chronological Membership 1644-1708

1. John Clarke - first pastor
2. Elizabeth Clarke
3. Mark Lucar
4. .Joseph Clarke
5. John Peckham
6. Nathaniel West
7. Mrs. West
8. William Weeden
9. Thomas Clarke
10. Willaim Vaughan
11. John Thorndon
12. Thomas Painter
13. Thomas Baker (Barker)
14. James Clarke
15. Jeremiah Clarke
16. Daniel Wightman

17. John Odlin
18. Jeremiah Weeden
19. .Joseph Card
20. John Greenman
21. Henry Clarke
22. Peleg Peckham
23. James Barber
24. Stephen Hookey
25. Timothy Peckham
26. Joseph Weeden
27. John Rhodes
28. James Brown
29. John Hammett
30. William Rhodes
31. Daniel Sabear
32. William Greenman
33.* Samuel Hubbard
    bp. Nov. 3, 1648
34 .* Tacey Hubbard
    bp. Nov. 3, 1648
35. Elenor Peckham -bp 1649
36. Obadiaah Holmes- ad 1651
37. John Crandall- ad 1651
38. Mary Torry -ad 1651
39. *Rachel Langworthy bp 1652
40. Andrew Langworthy
    bp Oct. 6, 1652
41. Ruth Hubbard bp Nov. 1652

42. Robert Burdick
    bp Nov. 16, 1652
43. Walter Clarke
    bp Nov 16, 1652
44. James Rogers
    bp Nov 16, 1652
45. Jack, a colored man
    bp Nov.16, 1652
46. Thomas Wilkins
    bp Jun 10, 1661
47. Mary Torry bp Jul 17,1661
48. Rachel Hubbard
    bp Jul 17, 1661
49. Bethuel Hubbard
    bp Sep 29, 1661
50. Philip Smith bp April 1662
51. John Maxson bp Apr 1662
52. *William Hiscox
    bp Jun 3, 1662
53. *Roger Baster-
    bp Jun 25, 1663;
  Stephen Mumford - bp 1665[1]

    admitted before 1664 [2]
54. **Nicholas Wild
55. **Mrs. Wild
56 **John Solomon
57.**Mrs. Solomon

Newport First Baptist Church 1644-   Newport RI
MF 1993.6   Microfilm Room
Seventh Day Baptist Historical Society Janesville WI

---

[1] Research indicates that Stephen Mumford and his wife were not members of the Newport Baptist Church but maintained membership in the Tewksbury Baptist Church in England which contained Sabbath keepers They became constiuent members of the Newport Seventh Day Baptist Church. One early record has the name Stephen Mumford inserted without a number after that of Roger Baster.

[2] Numbers 54, 55, 56, & 57, came to the Sabbath but later gave it up and did not join the SDB Church and even spoke against it.

SEVENTH DAY BAPTIST CHURCH 1671-1872,

"The following names of persons who became members previous to the year 1692, have been derived from the Church Records and other sources, and are as correct as our present means enable us to make the list, though the loss of the first book of records probably has deprived us of the knowledge of some names of persons who may have died previous to the before-mentioned date, and were therefore not on the list with which the the second volumn commences." There were an estimated 100 members

Members in 1692   * indicates charter members

*William Hiscox - b 1638,
    d May 24, 1704, first pastor
    for 33 yrs 1671-1704
*Rachel Langworthy d/o Samuel
    & Tacy Hubbard
      m Andrew Langworthy
Peter Barker
Mrs. _____Barker
Jos. Clarke Jr - m Bethiah Hubbard
Demaris Bliss d/o Gov. Arnold
    w/o John Bliss
James Babcock - bp 1678
Amy Collins
Hope Cove - Excom 1693
James Fowler
Jonathan Rogers -New London, CT
    bp 1675 family originated
    Rogerenes, Excom
Jas Rogers s/o James -
      New London CN, bp 1675
John Rogers bro/o Jonathan,
      New London CT -   bp 1675
James Rogers bro/o Jonathan,
      New London, CT bpt 1675
William Martin
Jos. Crandall s/o Eld. John
    Crandall -Dea. in Westerly,
    3rd pastor of Newport 1717,
    d Sep 12, 1737

Jonathan Sabin
John Maxson Sr.
Elizabeth Martin
Daniel Vernon
Freelove Barker
Mrs. _____ Vernon
Hannah Reed
Samuel Fox
*Tasa Hubbard w/o Samuel
    Hubbard - first person in
    New World to accept Sabbath
John Cottrell
Mary Gibson
Mary Rogers
Amy Smith Ward - w/o Thomas,
    gand d/o Roger Williams
Joseph Maxson - bp 1694
George Lanphere - bp 1678
Thomas West of Martha's Vineyard
Catharine Sabin
Peter Crandall
Elizabeth Millard
Peter Button - bp 1693
Rebecca Clarke
Bethiah Clarke
Sarah Martin
Naomi Rogers grandd/o Samuel
    Hubbard m Jonathan Rogers

Rachel Weeden
Thomas Burdick
Mr. ____ Henry
Mrs. ____ Henry
Robert Burdick
John Langworthy
John Randall
Elizabeth Langworthy
Job Babcock
Indian Japheth[3] - bp 1674,
    prob. first Indian Baptist
John Roads
Elizabeth Chase
Jos. Emerie
Esther Ayres, 2nd
Ebenezer Moon
Ruth Phillips
Jos. James
Ellen Rogers
Peter West
Ruth West
Elizabeth West
Elizabeth Barnes
Ruth Treby
Margaret Bennet
Edith Higgin
Ruth Burdick d/o Samuel & Tasy
    Hubbard - m   Robert Burdick
Esther Ayres

Sarah Arnold
Hannah Stowe
Elizabeth Randall
Elizabeth Emerie
Jane Babcock
Hannah Ayres
Sarah Rogers
Tobias Saunders
Hannah James
Mary Saunders
*Samuel Hubbard - b England
    1610, m Tasy Cooper of
    Dorcester, joined First Baptist
    Church of Newport 1648
*Roger Baster - then 50 yrs old,
    bachelor, blockmaker, d 1687
William Gibson - formerly of Bell
    Lane SDB Church London,
    2nd pastor 13 yrs, d 1717
Thomas Ward s/o of John of
    Gloucester Eng
John Thornton
John Crandall
*Stephen Mumford -formerly
    member of Tewkesbury
    (Natton) SDB Church Eng.
*Sister Mumford w/o Stephen

Newport RI (1692-1846) & First Hopkinton RI (1708-1714) Records
copy of earliest records by T. B. Stillman, W. S. Stillman, Joseph Stillman
CRR 19x.78   vault CRR
The Seventh Day Baptist Memorial: Quarterly Magazine
Vol. 1, July, 1852, No. 3, p. 121
Vol. 1., October, 1852, No. 4, p. 172
New York: Seventh Day Baptist Publishing Co. 1852

---

[3] According to some records, Japath was baptised in 1674 and is believed
to be the first native American to become a member of a Baptist Church.

Additional Members taken from the minutes of the Newport Church and the The Seventh Day Baptist Memorial: Quarterly Magazine Vol I and Vol 2,

John Maxson Jr - bp 1692
Judith Maxson - bp 1692
Tasa Maxson - bp 1692
Thomas Burdick - bp 1694
Martha Burdick - bp 1694
Joseph Clarke Jr - bp 1694
Dorothy Clark bp 1709
    d/o Joseph Clark Jr -
Henry Hall - bp 1697
Constant Hall - bp 1697
Mary Saunders - bp 1697
Mary Babcock - bp 1698
Francis Colegrove - bp 1698
Mrs. _____ Colegrove - bp 1698
Jeremiah Crandall - bp 1698
Benjamin Burdick - bp 1698
Samuel Beebe - bp 1698
Mary Crandall - bp 1698
Sarah Tift - bp 1699
Widow Jewell - bp 1699
Charity Dane - bp 1702
Mary Arnold d/o Thomas Ward,
    w/o Zion Arnold - bp 1704
James Halls - bp 1704

Sarah Halls w/o James - bp 1704
Mary Burdick w/o Benjamin -
    bp 1704
Elizabeth Gardiner - bp 1705
Indian Betty - bp 1705
Bethiah Hiscox - bp 1706
Thomas Clarke - bp 1706
Mary Roads - bp 1707
    w/o Theodore
Susanna Babcock - bp 1707
    w/o Oliver
William Clarke - bp 1707
Rebecca Larkin - bp 1707
Sarah Lanphere w/o Seth - bp 1707
Elizabeth Babcock - bp 1707
    w/o George
George Babcock - bp 1707
Margaret Champlin - bp 1708
    w/o William Jr
Samuel Clarke - bp 1708
Arnold Collins - no date, goldsmith
Henry Collins s/o Arnold - no date
Mary Champlin bp 1708
    w/o William Jr -

Members in 1708

William Gibson b. 1638 member of
    Bell Lane Church in England
    2nd pastor 1704-1717 d. 1717
Peter Barker
Hannah Read
John Reed
Ester Ayres
Joseph Emerie
Ebenezer Moon
Hannah Ayres

James Fowler
Philip Chase
Joseph James
Elizabeth Chase
Israel Barney
Ester Ayres, the younger
Peter West
Ruth Philips
William James
Ellen Rogers

William Martin
Sarah Rogers
Jonathan Sabin
Hannah James
Amy Collins
Catharine Sabin
Elizabeth West
Elizabeth Millard
Ruth Treby
Ruth West
Rachel Langworthy
Elizabeth Barney

Damaris Bliss
Margaret Bennet
Elizabeth Martin
Rebecca Clarke
Freelove Barker
Sarah Martin
Sarah Arnold
Hannah Stone
Mary Arnold
Rachel Weeden
Edith Higgin

Members Added Under Eld. Gibson's Ministry

Miriam Cook - bp 1709,
   m. Tuckerman
Patience Mecham - bp 1709
Joshua Weeks - bp 1710
Abigail Weeks - bp 1710
Esther Fleet - bp 1710
Elizabeth Vernon - bp 1710
Mary Ward - bp 1712
Phebe Excenior - bp 1712,
   m Vickers
Josiah Bliss bp 1712, d 1748
   s/o John & Demaris Arnold Bliss
Jonathan Weeden - bp 1715
Elizabeth Foster - bp 1715

Mary Davis - bp 1715
Abigail Bininger - bp 1715
Mary Ritter - bp 1715
Benjamin Chase Jr. - bp 1716
Mercy Chase - bp 1717
Sarah Belcher - bp 1717
Benjamin Chase - bp 1717
James Mott - bp 1717
Deborah Excenior - bp 1717
Edward Cartwright - bp 1717
Susanna Dennis - bp 1717
Samuel Thomas - no date

Added Duringthe pastorate of Elder Joseph Crandall 1717 --1737

Ann Marshall--bp 1718
Sarah Clarke - laying on
   hands 1718
William Bininger - bp 1718
Samuel Ritter - bp 1718
Jonathan Murphy -bp 1718
Joseph Barker, Jr. - bp 1719
Catherine Falaro - bp 1719

Ann Fleet - bp 1719
Mary Mott - bp 1719
Edward Fitz Randolph - 1719
Peggy Arnold (colored) -bp 1719
Elizabeth Collins - bp 1720
Sackfield West - bp 1720
Ruth West - bp 1720

78

Joseph Barney- bp 1721
Ruth Clarke - bp 1721
Sarah Thomas bp 1721
Constant Barney - received 1721
Hannah Pierce -received 1723
Widow Reed - received 1723
Joseph White - bp 1723
Anna Alesworth - bp 1724
Anna Anderson - bp 1725
Joshua Davis - received 1725
Hannah Fowler - received 1725
Hannah Hakes - received 1726
Mehetable Telford - bp 1727
Amy Higgins - bp 1727
Rachel Burdick - bp 1727

Abigail Crandall - bp 1727
    clerk, d Jan 20, 1785
Rachel Seaman - received 1728
Sarah Langworthy - bp 1828
Henry Collins - bp 1728
John Clarke - bp 1728
Lydia Rider - bp 1729
Abner Cartwright - bp 1733
Alethea Scisco - bp 1733
Martha Russel - received 1735
John Clarke - bp 1736
John Champlin - bp 1736
Abigail Hall -bp 1736
Reuben Peckham - received 1737
John Tanner - bp 1737, goldsmith,
deacon, trustee,

Members Added During the Interim between pastors 1738-1753

Mary Tanner - bp 1738
Michael Chase - bp 1740
Bathsheba McKee - bp 1741
Mary Davis - bp 1741
Ann Dodge - bp 1741
Elizabeth Stanbourch - bp 1741
Samuel Mariott - bp 1742
Elizabeth Mariott - bp 1742
Sarah Cartwright - bp 1743

Ann Anderson 2nd - bp 1743
Bryant Cartwright - bp 1743
George Bliss - bp 1743
Richard Hayward - received 1744
Samuel Barney - bp 1745
Jonathan Clarke - bp 1747
Gov. Richard Ward - bp 1753
Content Scofield - bp 1753

The Seventh Day Baptist Memorial: Quarterly Magazine
Vol. 2, January, 1853, No. 1, p. 26, 32, 35-7
New York: Seventh Day Baptist Publishing Co. 1853
CRR 1980.12   vault CRR
Newport RI Church Records 1708-1817
photocopy of microfilm owned by SDB Historical Society
original record book owned by Newport RI Historical Society

Members Added During Ministry of Elder John Maxson, the fourth pastor of the Newport Church. He was the grandson of the John Maxson,Sr. the first pastor of the Westerly or Hopkinton SDB Church and a nephew of Joseph Maxson the second pastor of that Church.

Elizabeth Smith - bp 1755
Michal Fish - bp 1755
Capt. Joshua Saunders - bp 1755
Freelove Saunders - bp 1755
Thomas West - bp 1756
Amey West w/o Thomas - bp 1756
Elizabeth Smith - bp 1756
Samuel Green - by letter 1757
Susanna Brand - bp 1757
Job Bennet Jr. - 1757
Mary Bennet - bp 1757
Sarah Greenman - bp 1758
Ann Maxson (wife/o Eld.) - bp 1758
Jonathan Maxson s/o Eld. - bp 1758
Dorothy Cartright - bp 1758
Sylvanus Greenman - bp 1759
Joseph Carpenter - bp 1759
Mrs. Carpenter - bp 1759
Catharine Cook - no date
Mary Jersey - bp 1761
Judge Henry Bliss - bp 1762
Mary Bliss - bp 1762
Joseph Southwick - bp 1762
Grace Rogers- bp 1763
        w/o David -
Jane Lewis of Portsmith - bp 1763
Barsheba Barker of Middletown
    bp 1763

Capt. William Bliss of
    Middletown-b 1728,
    bp 1764 at Green End
   m 1750 Barbara Phillips d. 1775
   m Jan 9, 1780 Elizabeth Ward
    d/o Richard Ward,
    5th pastor d May 4, 1808
Abigail Cartright -bp 1764
    d/o Bryant of Tisbrey on
    Martha's Vineyard -
Barbary Bliss - bp 1764
    w/o Capt William
Elizabeth Mariott - bp 1765
    d/o Samuel
Elizabeth Sabin - bp 1767
    d/o Henry
Lydia MacDonald - bp 1767
    d/o Henry Sabin
Jane Brightson - bp 1767
    d/o Henry Sabin
Mrs. Shairman w/o Elisha - bp
Charles Ward - bp 1767
    s/o Samuel -
Judah Cartright - bp 1767
Martha McCloud - bp 1768
Elizabeth Clarke - bp 1769
    d/o Lawrence
Elizabeth Clarke- bp 1769
    d/o Henry Bliss, w/o James
Mary Shreve widow bp 1870
    d/o Samuel Green -
John Maxson - bp 1770

Ann Maxson d/o Eld. - bp 1770
Elizabeth Clarke - bp 1770
Benedict Bliss s/o Henry - bp 1770
Ebenezer David s/o Enoch -
  bp 1770, ordained 1755
Patience Bennet - bp 1770
  w/o Col. Job
Mary Bliss d/o Henry - bp 1770
Elizabeth Bliss bp 1770 d/o
  Capt. William of Middletown
Barbary Bliss bp 1770 d/o
  Capt. William of Middletown
Brenton Bliss bp. 1770
  s/o Henry
Content Maxson d/o
  Elder Maxson

Scipio Tanner, bp. 1771
  Negro servant of Widow Flaggs
Young negro servant of
  Dea. Tanner
Arthur Flaggs bp. 1771
Mary Hastie ad. by letter 1773
Elizabeth Larkin bp. 1773
Martha Pendelton bp. 1773
Elizabeth Ward - bp 1773
  d/o Richard.
Hannah Hazard bp. 1774
  w/o George of S. Kingston
Esther Fish bp 1774
William Chamlin bp. 1775
Ann Rodman bp. 1776
Mrs. Flagg bp. 1776

Living Members 1784

Elder William Bliss - ordained
1779, pastor 1778-1808
Dea. John Tanner
Job Bennet - d 1784
Reuben Packham
William Champlin
Jonathan Maxson
William Saunders
John Maxson
Ann Cartright
Joseph Carpenter
Dolly Fry
Scipio Tanner, Negro
Catharine Burdick
Arthur Flagg, Negro
Ann Babcock
Esther Fish
Lydia Clarke
Barbara Barker

Elizabeth Smith
Elizabeth Larkin
Mary Hastie
Sarah Greenman
Amy Bissel
Elizabeth Packham
Elizabeth Weeden
Ann Wilcox
Mary Shreve
Prude Saunders
Freelove Tanner
Martha Pendleton
Sarah C. Bliss
Content Maxson
Mary Pearse
Naomi Coggeshall
Mary Bliss
Mrs. Herrick
Patience Bennet

81

Mrs. Carpenter
Elizabeth Bliss wife/o Elder
Barbara Bliss d/o Elder

Elizabeth Bliss d/o Elder
Three colored women

Members Added During Ministry of William Bliss

Ann Bissel - bp 1780
Anne Wilcox bp 1781
William Saunders - bp 1782
Prude Saunders - bp 1780
Elizabeth Weeden, widow -
   bp 1782
Sarah Thurston - bp 1782
Naomi Coggeshall - bp 1782
   w/o Elisha
Peggy Flagg d/o Arthur - bp 1783
Mary Gears w/o John - bp 1783
Charity Cuzzens, colored -
   bp 1783
Thomas Ward Bliss bp 1783
   s/o William -
Mary Maxson - bp 1785
   d/o William
Sarah Bliss d/o William - bp 1785
Arnold Bliss of Ponegansett, s/o
William -bp 1786,ordained 1803
 George Bliss - bp 1786
   s/o William
Frances McDonald - bp 1786
Violet Flagg d/o Arthur - bp 1786
Margaret Irish - bp 1787
Mary Parker of Bedford- bp 1788
   w/o Avery -
John Pickens of Fair Haven
   - bp 1788
Sarah Adsett widow from Bedford
   bp 1788
Sarah Wait - bp 1788
   widow from Pongansett

Patty Cushman of Ponegansett
   bp 1788
Patience Easton - bp 1789
Clarke Burdick - bp 1794
Lydia Burdick - bp 1794
Sarah Maxson w/o John - bp 1794
Margaret Crandall - bp 1795
   w/o Philip
Caleb Maxson s/o John - bp 1796
Rosanna Arthur - bp 1796
Phoebe Arthur - bp 1796
Jonathan Maxson bp 1799
   s/o Jonathan -
William Bliss Maxson - bp 1799
   s/o Caleb,
   grand s/o Eld. William Bliss
John Bliss s/o Eld. - bp 1801
Elizabeth Bliss - bp
   w/o Arnold 1801
Abigail Bliss bp 1802
   w/o William of New Bedford
Henry Burdick - bp 1802
George Clarke Jr - bp 1802
Jonathan Burdick - bp 1802
Hannah Bliven - bp 1802
   w/o Henry
Henry Bliven - bp 1803
Nancy Thurston - bp 1803
Daniel Burdick - bp 1802
Susanna Burdick - bp 1802
John D. Moranville - bp 1803
Catharine Adams - bp 1803
James Mariott - bp 1803

Sarah Stacy - bp 1803
Abigail Sears - bp 1803
Amy Bliss- bp 1804
  w/o William Bliss of Bedford
Elizabeth Bliss- bp 1804
  d/o Eld. Arnold
Arnold Bliss Jr bp 1804
  s/o Eld. Arnold -
Clarke Bliss - bp 1806
John Thurston - bp 1806
Dwelly Moranville - bp 1806
Catharine Maxson - bp 1806
Betsey Fry - bp 1806
Jeremiah Bliss - bp 1806
Polly Bliss - bp 1806Aldredge
Saunders - bp 1806
John Maxson - bp 1806
Elizabeth A. Bliss - bp 1806
Barbara Bliss - bp 1806
Sarah Bliss - bp 1806
Sarah Allen - bp 1806
Polly Pearce - bp 1806
Rachael Moranville - bp 1806
Joseph Bliven - bp 1806
Charles Burdick - bp 1806

Deborah Green - bp 1806
Mary Bliss - bp 1806
Mary Barker - bp 1806
Mary Maxson - bp 1806
Elizabeth Champlin - bp 1806
Abigail Maxson - bp 1806
Adam Burdick - bp 1806
Henry Bliss - bp 1806
Keturah Clarke - bp 1806
Phoebe Clarke - bp 1806
Anna Cartright - bp 1806
Edward Allen - bp 1806
George Clarke - received 1806
Keturah Clarke - received 1806
Augustus Clarke - received 1806
Jedediah Clarke - received 1806
Benjamin Thurston Bliss -
  received 1806
Mary Burdick - bp 1806
Bathsheba Burdick - bp 1806
Richard Closon - bp 1806
Cuffee Benson - bp 1807
Arthur Flagg Jr - bp 1807
Sanford Harvey - received 1807
Charlotty Davis - received 1807
William Bliss 2nd - bp 1807

Members Living in 1808

Caleb Maxson
Mary Bliss
Mary Bliss
Jonathan Maxson
Jonathan Maxson
John Maxson
William B. Maxson
Scipio Tanner
Henry Burdick
Arthur Flagg

George Clarke
Arnold Bliss
Jonathan Burdick
Henry Bliven
George Bliss
Clarke Burdick
Daniel Burdick
John D. Moranville
Mary Gears
James Marriott

Violet Flagg
Arnold Bliss Jr
Mary Bliss
Lydia Burdick
Clarke Bliss
Sarah Maxson
John L. Thurston
Margaret Crandall
Daniel Moranville
Phoebe Benson
Jeremiah Bliss
Rosanna Flagg
John O. Saunders
Elizabeth Bliss
John Maxson
Abigail Bliss
Edward Allen
Hannah Bliss
Adam Burdick
Nancy Thurston
Henry Bliss
Susannah Burdick
Jedediah Clarke
Abigail Sears
George Clarke
Elizabeth Bliss
Augustus Clarke
Amy Bliss
Benjamin T. Bliss
Catharine Dart
Richard Closon
Catherine Saunders
Cuffee Benson
Elizabeth Closen
Arthur Flagg Jr

Sanford Hervy
Elizabeth E. Bliss
Joseph Bliven
Barbara P. Murphy
Charles Burdick
Sarah Stillman
William Bliss
Sarah Allen
Polly Pearce
Ann Cartright
Rachael D. Moranville
Catharine Burdick
Deborah Green
Content Scofield
Mary Maxson
Bathsheba Barker
Mary Clarke
Elizabeth Peckham
Mary Alger
Mary Bliss
Elizabeth Champlin
Elizabeth Greenman
Barbara Bliss
Keturah Clarke
Content Maxson
Phoebe Clarke
Elizabeth Larkin
Ann C. Way
Ann Wilcox
Keturah Clarke
Elizabeth Bliss
Mary Burdick
Sarah C. Bliss
Bathsheba Burdick
Naomi Coggeshall
Charlotty Davis

Members Added During Ministry of Elder Henry Burdick 1808-1843

Ruth Clarke - received 1810
Ann Rogers - bp 1813
Clarke Burdick - bp 1813
Henry Burdick - bp 1813
Susanna Burdick - bp 1813
Enos Burdick - bp 1813
Susanna Bliss - bp 1813
Susanna Hiscox - bp 1816
Susanna Cotrell - bp 1816
Mary Congdon - 1817
Nathaniel Cotrell - bp 1817
Ruth Bliss - bp 1818
Eliza Burdick - bp 1820

Ruth Burdick - bp 1820
Mary Barker - bp 1820
Sarah A. Burdick - bp 1820
Isaiah Barker - bp 1820
Amy Bliss - bp 1822
Martha Bliss - bp 1823
Ebenezer D. Bliss - bp 1823
Benjamin Barker - bp 1828
Ichabod Burdick - bp 1828
Patience Burdick - bp 1828
Julian Kenyon - bp 1828
Henrietta Burdick - bp 1828
Ira Stillman - bp 1830

**Seventh Day Baptist Memorial: Quarterly Magazine
Vol 2, April, 1853, No. 2, p. 80-1, 84-5, 89-91, 92-3,94
New York: Seventh Day Baptist Publishing Society 1853
CRR 1980.12 vault CRR
Newport RI Church Records 1708-1817
photocopy of microfilm owned by Seventh Day Baptist Historical
Society
original record book owned by Newport Historical Society**

Members	Members Added
Elder Bliss Jr	Mrs. Ingram - ad 1843
William Bliss	Elder Lucius Crandall - ad by letter
Arron Rogers	1843, dis
Nathaniel Cottrell	Edmund D. Barker - ad 1843
Lydia Burdick	John Congdon - ad 1843
Sarah Maxson	Catharine D. Barker - ad 1843
Phoebe Benson	Alice Weeden - ad by letter 1843
Rosanna Flagg	Susan Allen - restored 1843 & dis
Catharine Dart	Sarah B. Burdick - ad 1843
Barbary P. Murphy	Eliza Luther - ad 1843
Sarah Allen	William Augustus Weeden -
Mary Clarke	ad by letter 1843
Mary Alger	Catharine Weeden - ad by letter 1843
Abigail Maxson	John C. Burdick - ad by letter 1844
Phebe Clarke	John E. G. Weeden -
Bathsheba Sisson	ad by letter 1845
Eunice Burdick	George W. Weeden -
Susanna Burdick - d	ad by letter 1845
Susanna Cottrell	Peleg Weeden - ad by letter 1845
Henrietta Burdick - excom	Sarah T. Congdon
Keturah C. Barker	Lebbeus Cottrell -
Phebe More	ad by letter 1845, dis
Rosanna Taylor	Eld. Charles M. Lewis -
	ad by letter 1845
	Elisa A. Lewis - ad by letter 1845

Deaths

Charles W. Burdick - d Oct 31, 1841; 50 yrs
Elder Henry Burdick - d Oct 30, 1846; 77 yrs
Susanna Cottrell - d May 18, 1846; 80 yrs
Rosanna Taylor - d Oct 25, 1847; 75 yrs

CRR 19x.79   vault
Newport RI Church Record 1843-1846 original
IMS:1996

Part Three

Mother Hubbard's Cupboard
Is Not Bare
Genealogy of the Samuel and Tacy Hubbard family
to the third or fourth generation

The numbering of the decendents shows relationship with the alphabetic listing for the children of Samuel and Tacy Hubbard and the numerical numbers for each succeeding generation. For example: C shows that Ruth Hubbard is the third child of Samuel and Tacy Hubbard; C4 indicates that Deborah was the fourth child of Ruth and Robert Burdick; C43 states that Joseph Crandall, Jr was the third child of Deborah Burdick Crandall and Joseph Crandall; and C431 that Joseph III was their fist child. The bracketed letter and number after a spouses name shows relationship within the extended family, thus a [D11] shows that Joseph Crandall's wife, Ann Langworthy, was a grandaughter of Ruth's sister, Rachel Hubbard.

Footnotes are given to identify some of the spouses' descent from other individuals who were significant in the history of the early Seventh Day Baptist community or history.

Samuel Hubbard b. 1610 d. abt. 1689 m. 1636
Tacy Cooper b. abt. 1609

A. Naomi Hubbard d. *10 days old*
B . Naomi Hubbard d. 6yr old
C. Ruth Hubbard b. abt.1640 d. 1692 m. 1655   Robert Burdick [1]
  C1 Thomas Burdick b.abt.1656 d. 1732 m. abt.1690 Martha
    C11 Martha Burdick b. abt.169__ m. 4/24/1729 William Stewart
      C111 William Stewart b. 10/19/1734 m.1/30/175_ Mary Lanphere
      C112 Martha Stewart b. 11/1736.

---

[1] Robert Burdick was baptised as a member of the First Baptist Church of Newport on 11/16/1652 and represented the church in its struggle against the persecution of dissenters from the established church in Massachusetts. He and Tobias Saunders were arrested in 1662 and sentenced to two years in Boston jail but were eventually realeased in a prisoner exchange. He was among the earliest settlers of the western section of Rhode Island. He was listed as a member of the Newport Seventh Day Baptist Church in its 1692 record. He died Oct. 25, 1692.

C12 Robert Burdick b. abt.1698   m.   Dorcas Lewis
    C121 Daniel Burdick b. 9/11/1721 m. 1746   Martha Wilcox
    C122 Martha Burdick b 10/11/1723 m. 1/25/1741 John Covey
    C123 Robert Burdick b. 1/2/1724 m. 9/11/1744   Jane Bennett
    C124 Dorcas Burdick b. 10/5/1726 m. 7/8/1752 Joshua Salisbury
    C125 Ruth Burdick b. 3/10/1728 m.   ____Smith?
    C126 Ephraim Burdick b. 1/6/1730
    C127 Mary Burdick b. 10/3/1732 m. Richard Bennet?
    C128 Hannah Burdick b. 9/17/1734 m. 2/9/1763 Rev. Nathan Sisson
    C129 Matthew Burdick b. 12/23/1738 m. Anna Jewett
    C12(10) Margaret Burdick b. 1740 m 6/24/1758 Amos Dickens
    C12(11) Jesse Burdick b. 8/16/1742 m.   ____Brock
  C13 Thomas Burdick b abt. 1695   m. (1) ____
    C131 Thomas Burdick b. abt. 1720 m. 12/6/1742   Sarah Allen
                       m. (2) 5/1/1723   Abigail Richmond
    C132   Simeon Burdick b. 17__ m. 9/20/174   Isabel Saunders
    C133 Abigail Burdick b. 17__ m. 11/5/1750 Capt. Isaac Hall
      C134 Edmund Burdick b. 17__ m. 4/23/1749   Thankful Enos
    C135 Jonathan Burdick b. 17__ d. 1764 m. 8/2/1761 Patience Bliven
    C136 Elizabeth Burdick b. 1739 d.1794 m. 3/1/1757 Jonathan Brown
                       m (3) 2/9/1763   Penelope Rhodes
    C137 Martha Burdick b.   William Bennett
  C14 Mary Burdick   b. abt. 169__ d. aft. 1740 m Jeremiah Clarke
    C141 Jeremiah Clarke b.
    C142 Peleg Clarke b.
    C143 Sarah Clarke b.   m.   Joseph Lewis
    C144 Katherine Clarke b.   m. 10/1/1752   John Millard
  C15 Comfort Burdick 17__ d.7/22/1728 m. 5/18/1721 William York
    C151 William York b. 2/22/1728
  C16 Samuel Hubbard Burdick b. aft 1772 m. 11/5/1731 Avis Maxson
                                [F1(10)]
    C161 Rev. John Burdick b. 1732 m. (1) 11/23/1752 Sibbil
                              Cheeseborough
                  (2) 3/9/1788 Thankful Clarke [F342]
    C162 Samuel Hubbard Burdick b.8/19/1734 m. 10/31/1757 Amie
                                  MacCoon
    C163 Abraham Burdick b. 6/16/1737 m.   Amy Brown
    C164 Avis Burdick b.5/29/1739 m. 3/18/1756 Wm Robinson
    C165 Amos Burdick b. 7/6/1741 m. 2/4/1761 Elizabeth Nichols
    C166 Margaret Burdick b. 174__ m. 4/7/1763 Joshua Coon
C2 Naomi Burdick b. abt.1658   m. (1) 3/2/1678   Jonathan Rogers[2]
                      (2) 3/11/1703   John Keeny
  C21 Ruth Rogers b. 1678   m.   William Beebe
    C211 Stephen Beebe   m. 11/16/1716   Mary Leach

_____

[2] Jonathan Rogers was the son of James Rogers, the founder of the
Rogerene off-shoot in New London, Connecticut.

C212 Mary Beebe   m. (prob)   James Beebe
C213 William Beebe   m. 6/9/1726   Jerusha Beebe
C214 Ezekiel Beebe
C215 Lydia Beebe   m. 12/7/1727   Ezekiel Sawyer
C22 Elizabeth Rogers b 1681 m. 1/8/1702   James Smith
   C221 James Smith b. 3/25/1703 d. infancy
   C222 James Smith b. 8/20/1704
   C223 Bathsheba Smith b. 1705 d.7/31 1755 m.   Daniel Gardner
   C224 Richard Smith   m.   Abigail Gardner
   C225 Jonathan Smith   m. 8/24/1732   Sarah Gardner
   C226 Panalah Smith   b. 7/30/1708
   C227 Samuel Smith
   C228 Ebenezer Smith b. 2/26/1710   m. (1) _____ Gardner?
                        m. (2)   Mary _____
   C229 Anna Smith
   C22(10) Mindwell Smith b. 4/22/1714
C23 Naomi Rogers b.1689 d.10/20/1725 m 2/25/1708 Benjamin Fox
C231 Benjamin Fox b. 8/29/1715 m 11/7/1745 Abigail Brockway
C232 John Fox   m. 3/19/1746   Mary Pierce
C233 Jesse Fox
C234 Thomas Fox
C235 Sarah Fox   m.(prob)   Jedediah Brockway
C236 Lucy Fox ____   d. 8/31/1750 m.   Charles Thompson
C237 Lydia Fox   m. (prob.)   Peter Douglas
C238 Hannah Fox b.1738 d. 9/29/1793 m. 1/22/1755 Michael Powers
C239 Naomi Fox
C23(10) Margaret Fox
     four others by second wife, Daniel, Stephen, Joseph and Tacy

C24 Content Rogers b. 1688 d. 1768 m. (1)5/1/1707 Jonathan Maxson[3]
                     m   (2)   Richard Lake
                     m   (3) 1/24/1756   Timothy Peckham
   C241 Jonathan Maxson b. 1/17/1708
   C242 Content Maxson b.1/28/1709 m (1)7/7/1731James Babcock
                  (2) 12/22/1742   William Hiscox [F511]
   C243..Joseph Maxson b. 1/14/1712
   C244 John Maxson b.3/2/1714 m.10/22/1736 Tacy Rogers[C256]
   C245 Naomi Maxson b. 5/6/1716
   C246 Samuel Maxson b.7/20/1718d.1796 m1/13/1742 Ruth Rogers
   C247 Caleb Maxson b. 11/1/1721 d. abt. 1752
   C248 Mary Maxson b. 11/20/1723 m. 5/12/1748   Joshua Chase

---

[3] Jonathan Maxson was the son of John Maxson and Mary Mosher. Two of his brothers and two sisters married into the Hubbard line: Rev. John Jr married Bethiah' daughter, Judith Clarke [F1]; Rev. Joseph Maxson married Tacy Burdick [C8]; Dorothy married Joseph Clarke [F2] ; and Hannah married Hubbard Burdick [C(10)]

C25 Jonathan Rogers b 1690 d. 1777 m. 11/24/1711 Judith Potter [4]
   C251 Judith Rogers b. 11/30/1712 m. 1747   Thomas Potter
   C252 Jonathan Rogers b. 11/24/1714 m.(1) 1737 Hannah
                                          Hiscox [F58]
                          m. (2)   Sarah Newbury
   C253 Peace Rogers b. 8/30/1716
   C254 Nathan Rogers b. 5/6/1718 m. (1)   Martha Davis [F143]
                       m.(2)   Hannah Crandall
   C255 David Rogers b. 3/8/1719 m. (1)   Grace Lester
                m. (2) Judith (Maxson) Greene [F157]
   C256 Tacy Rogers   m. Elder John Maxson [C244]
   C257 Bethia Rogers b. 4/1/1725 m. Elder John Davis Jr. [F144]
   C258 Hannah Rogers b. 12/25/1727 m. 3/5/1745 Elisha
                                     Stillman [C457]
   C259 Mary Rogers b. 5/26/1731
C26 Rachel Rogers b. 1692 d. 1745 m. 11/__/1714 Samuel Fox Jr
   C261 Jonathan Fox b. 10/5/1715   unmarried
   C262 Hannah Fox b. 5/4/171 m. 3/13/1737 David Lester (2nd wife)
   C263 Samuel Fox b. 6/29/1719 d. 1/__/1752
   C264 James Fox b. 7/21/1722
   C265 Rachel Fox b. 5/24/1724 d. 8/30/1736 m.1735 David Lester
                                      (1st wife)
   C266 Naomi Fox b. 4/31/1731 m. (1)Amos Beebe (2) Ebenezer Rogers
   C267 Bathsheba Fox b. 8/31/1733 m.   James Ryon
C27 Katherine Rogers b. 1694 m. 4/5/ 1720 William Brookfield, Jr.
   C271 Uriah Brookfield b. 5/7/1722
   C272 Stephen Brookfield b. 8/30/1724
   C273 Charles Brookfield b. 7/27/1726
   C274 Elizabeth Brookfield b. 7/31/1728
C3 Ruth Burdick b. abt.1660 d. aft 1730 m abt..1682 John Phillips
   C31 John Phillips b. abt.1683
   C32 Michael Phillips b. abt.1685
   C33 Barbara Phillips b. 3/15/1687 d. 1726 m.11/8/1711 Isaac Peckham
      C331 John Peckham b. 5/1/1712 d.1787 m.12/25/1735 Deborah Sweet
      C332 Isaac Peckham b. 10/20/1713
      C333 Sarah Peckham b. 10/6/1715
      C334 Benjamin Peckham b 10/19/1717
      C335 Ruth Peckham b. 7/12/1719
      C336 Clement Peckham b. 5/20/1721
      C337 Stephen Peckham b. 3/6/1722
      C338 son b. 7/11/1725

---

[4] It was through Judith Potter that the 1549 Cranmer Bible was preserved and came to the SDB Historical Society. This was the Testment of which Samuel Hubbard wrote:" *Now 1675 I have a testament of my grandfather Cocke' s printed in 1549 which he hid in his bedstraw lest it be burnt in Queen Mary's days.*"

C34 Benjamin Phillips
C35 William Phillips
C36 Samuel Phillips
C4 Deborah Burdick b.abt.1662 d.1687 m. abt.1681 Joseph Crandall[5]
  C41 John Crandall. abt. 1682 d. 1767 m. (1) _____
                                    (2) Hannah _____
                                    (3) Elizabeth Lewis
    C42 Lydia Crandall b. abt. 1683   m.   Robert Babcock
      C421 Mary Babcock b. 8/31/1702
      C422 Lydia Babcock b. 11/3/1703 m.   Roger Elderton
      C423 Robert Babcock b. 5/8/1706
      C424 Elihu Babcock b. 6/5/1708
      C425 Sarah Babcock b. 3/18/1710
      C426 Patience Babcock b. 12/23/1711
      C427 Simeon Babcock b.10/17/1714 m. 10/5/1736 Abigail Hudson
      C428 Ezekiel Babcock b. 6/22/1716 m.   Eunice Billings
      C429 Joseph Babcock b. 4/9/1718
      C42(10) Remember Babcock b. 2/11/1720
    C43 Joseph Crandall b. 168__ m. 2/15/1715 Ann Langworthy [D11]
      C431 Joseph Crandall b. 1/17/1716 m. (1) 5/2/1736 Edith Hiscox F53]
                              (2) m 12/13/1738 Elizabeth Crandall
      C432 James Crandall b.5/12/1719 m. (1)2/27/1742 Demaris Kenyon
                              (2) Mrs. Elizabeth Saunders
      C433 William Crandall b. 8/6/1721 m. /12/1747Deborah Crandall
      C434 Simeon Crandall b. 1/15/1724 m.6/23/1745 Mary Sweet
      C435 Joshua Crandall b.10/15/1727 m. 9/18/1750 Eunice Kenyon
      C436 Ezekiel Crandall b. 11/21/1730 d. young
      C437 Ann Crandall b. 7/21/1733 m. 12/14/1752 James Rhodes
      C438 Benjamin Crandall b11/20/1736 m.6/26/1758 AliceKenyon
    C44 Mary Crandall b. abt. 1686 m. 1706   Nathaniel Wells
      C441 Naomi Wells b. 5/11/1707 m. 9/15/1726   Peter Kenyon
      C442 Elizabeth Wells b. 6/9/1710
      C443 Jonathan Wells b. 6/22/1712 m. 11/29/1734 Elizabeth Maxson
                                                      [C87]
      C444 Tacy Wells b. 1/4/1715 m. Capt Hubbard Burdick [C92]
      C445 Ruth Wells b. 9/6/1717

---

[5] Rev. Joseph Crandall was the son of Elder John Crandall who was born in England in 1612 and came to America in 1634. John Crandall was one of the founders of Providence and was one of the original purchasers of the Misquamicut region from which Hopkinton was formed. He was the first pastor of the Baptists Congregation in that area and represented the Baptists in their struggle with the Puritans of Massachusetts.He was arrested along with Rev. John Clarke and Obadiah Holmes in 1651. Rev. John became to first pastor of the Westerly (Hopkinton) branch of the Newport Seventh Day Baptist Church.

C446 Thomas Wells b. 1719
C447 Deborah Wells m.   Thomas Partelo
C45 Deborah Crandall b.abt. 1688 d. 1760-62 m. 4/3/1706 Dr. George
                                                        Stillman
    C451 Deborah Stillman b. 1/11/1707 m. 4/13/1741 Benjamin
                                                        Tanner
    C452 Nathaniel Stillman b. 5/2/1709 d. infancy
    C453 Mary Stillman b. 9/27/1711 d. 2/26/1789
    C454 George Stillman b. 2/14/1714 m.11/3/1737 Mary Burdick
    C455 Joseph Stillman b. 12/5/1716 m. 6/17/1739 Mary Maxson
                                                        [F132]
    C456 John Stillman b. 6/14/1719 m. 12/12/1745   Mary Clarke
    C457 Elisha Stillman b. 4/25/1722 m. (1) 3/5/1745 Hannah Rogers
                                                        [C457]
                        (2) 1/3/1759 Mary Davis [F149]
                        (3)   Elizabeth Burdick
    C458 Benjamin Stillman b 1/25/ 1725 m.2/28/175 Mary Saunders
C46 Thankful Crandall b abt. 1685 d. 1712 m.   Stephen Saunders
    C461 Thankful Saunders b. 1712
C47 Tacy Crandall b. abt. 1692 m. 3/3/1717   John Lewis
C48 Jane Crandall b 1694 d. 12/_/1730 m. (1) 12/8/1718 Cyrus Richmond
                        (2) 3/27/1734   Phoebe Mott
    C481 Lydia Richmond b. 11/4/1719 m. 3/30/1744   John Allen
    C482 Elizabeth Richmond b. 7/30/1722
    C483 John Richmond b. 6/19/1724
    C484 Ann Richmond b. 9/1/1726
    C485 Cyrus Richmond b. 12/8/1730
C5 Roger Burdick b. abt.1664   d. before 9/25/83
C6 Benjamin Burdick b.abt.1666 d. 4/23/1741 m. (1) abt.1698 Mary Reynolds
                        (2) after 1718   Mrs Jane Shelly
C61 Mary Burdick b. 7/26/1699   m. 3/12/1718 John Lewis Jr
C62 Rachel Burdick b. 7/5/1701   m   (1)   Thomas Sisson
                        (2) 1743   Walter Clarke
C63 Peter Burdick b. 8/5/1703 m. 4/17/1726 Desire Reynolds
C64 Benjamin Burdick b. 11/25/1705 m. Rebecca Bennett
C65 John Burdick b. 3/24/1708 m. 10/21/1730 Rebecca Thompson
C66 David Burdick b. 2/24/ 1710 m. 7/25/1733 Mary Thompson
C67 William Burdick b. 6/12/1713 m.   Sarah Edwards
C68 Elisha Burdick b. 9/22/1716 m. 2/25/1739   Mary Slack
C7 Samuel Burdick b. abt.1668 d. 4/_/1756 m. 169__ Mary Foster
C71 Mary Burdick   m. 2/27/1717   Peter Crandall
C72 Samuel Burdick b. abt.1696 m.   Tacy Maxson [C83]
    C721 Samuel Burdick b. 172__ m.   Mary Cross
    C722 Mary Burdick b. 1720 m.11/3/1737 George Stillman[C454]
    C723 Sarah Burdick b. 11/18/1725 m.10/30/1746 John Maxson Jr
                                                . [F161]
    C724 Christopher Burdick b. ___
    C725 Deborah Burdick b 174__ m   Benjamin Teft

C726 Jesse Burdick b. 173__ d. 1812 unmar.
C727 Joshua Burdick b. 173__   m.   Mary Lamb
C73 Thomas Burdick m.   Dorothy Maxson [F17]
   C731 Zaccheus Burdick b. 2/28/1734 d. 1809 m. 2/19/1759
                                                                   Elizabeth Smith
   C732 Susanna Burdick b. abt.1736 d. 1794 m. 1759 Benjamin Austin
   C733 Zebediah Burdick   m.   Isabel _____
   C734 Elias Burdick m (1) 1/17/1754   Hannah Cottrell
                   (2) 8/23/1764   Elizabeth Cottrell
   C735 Carey Burdick m. 12/27/1754   Dorcas Cottrell
   C736 Thomas Burdick m.   Abigail Allen
C74 Deborah Burdick b. 17__ m. 1730   Joseph Champlin [F63]
C75 Edward Burdick b. abt.1705 m. 11/26/1730 Sarah Clarke[F81]
   C751 James Burdick b. 1731   m.   Catherine Vars
   C752 Mary Burdick b. 17__m. 8/14/1764 Newman Herring
   C753 Anna Burdick b. 8/16/1733 m.   Azariah Crandall
   C754 Mercy Burdick b. 17__
   C755 Prudence Burdick b. abt.1734 d. 9/_1807 m.1754 Joshua
                                                       Whitford
   C756 Elizabeth Burdick b. 11/17/___m. 1755   Isaac Vars
   C757 Sarah Burdick b. 17__
C76 Tacy Burdick b. abt. 1710 m 6/12/1732   Benjamin Frink
   C761 John Frink b. 10/26/1732 m. 11/22/1750   Anna Pendleton
   C762 Samuel Frink b. 10/24/1734 m. 7/27/1756 Prudence Wilcox
   C763 Amos Frink b. 1/18/1737 m. 2/4/1759   Mary Fitch
   C764 Joseph Frink b. 6/20/1739
   C765 Prentice Frink b. 7/31/1741 m. 11/13/1763   Desire Frink
   C766 Prudence Frink b. 3/18/1744
   C767 Tacy Frink b. 9/22/1748 (Twin to Asa)
   C768 Asa Frink b. 9/22/1748 d. 12/11/1834 m. (1) _____
                 m. (2) 10/4/1758 Mrs. Theda (York) Brown
   C769 Oliver Frink b. 9/4/1751

C8 Tacy Burdick b. abt.1670 m. abt.1670   Rev. Joseph Maxson
   C81 Joseph Maxson b. 3/10/1692 m. abt.1715   Bethiah Maxson [F13]
        See F13 for their children
   C82 Capt John Maxson b_____ d. 1775 m (1)   Hannah Maxson [F15]
                   (2)   Martha Lewis
   C83 Tacy Maxson m. 172__   Samuel Burdick Jr. [C72]
        See C72 for their children
   C84 Mary Maxson   m. 1724   Geoffrey Champlin
   C85 Ruth   Maxson   m. 1727   Thomas or Rouse Babcock
   C86 Judith Maxson m. 1724   Matthew Randall
   C87 Elizabeth Maxson m. 11/29/1734   Jonathan Wells [C443]
C9 Robert Burdick b. 1674 m.(1) 1/4/1700   Rebecca Foster
             (2) 1733   Mrs Hannah Saunders
   C91 Robert Burdick b. abt. 1701 m. 12/31/1730 Susannah Clarke [F92]
   C92 Hubbard Burdick b. abt. 1714 m. abt. 1734 Tacy Wells [C444]

C93 Jonathan Burdick b. abt.1708 d.1791 m. abt.1729   Judith Clarke
                                                                [F91]
C94 Ebenezer Burdick b.170_d. 1764 m. (1) 1/21/1730 Elizabeth Stewart
                              (2) 2/14/1740   Mary Dyer
C95 Joshua Burdick b. 171_d. 1800 m. 12/25/1734   Abigail Lanphere
C96 Benjamin Burdick b. 171___ m. 12/28/1737   Elizabeth Tanner
C97 Joseph Burdick b. 17_d. after 1785 m. (1) 8/13/1735 Tase Clarke
                              (2)   Elizabeth _____
C98 Rebecca Burdick b. 17___ m.   3/18/1736   James Reynolds
C99 Susannah Burdick b. 170_d. before 1742 m.1/11/1727 William Hiscox
                                                                [F51]
C9(10) Elizabeth Burdick   m. before 1729   Joseph Langworthy

C(10) Hubbard Burdick b. abt.1676 m. abt. 1714   Hannah Maxson
    C(10)1 Hubbard Burdick b.11/24/1716 m. 11/1/1743   Avis Lewis
        C(10)1 Hubbard Burdick
        C(10)2 Hannah Burdick b.174__   m.   Abraham Utter
        C(10)3 John Burdick b. 174__   m. (1)   Martha _____
                              (2)   Mehitaba _____
        C(10)4 Caleb Burdick   m.   Hulda _____
        C(10)5 Reuben Burdick
        C(10)6.Amos Burdick
        C(10)7 James Burdick
        C(10)8 Freedom Burdick
        C(10)9 Peleg Burdick b. 5/10/1761 m. 11/30/1780 Catherine Millard
        C(10)(10) Pardon Burdick   m.   Sabrah _____
        C(10)(11) Lewis Burdick b. 1/10/1761 m 178____   Eunice Satterlee
        C(10)(12) Latham Burdick
    C(10)2 Nathan Burdick b.2/19/1719 m 10/14/1743 Goodeth Maxson
                                                                [F155]
        C(10)21 Zillimus Burdick b. 5/30/1745
        C(10)22 Sylvanus Burdick b. 9/17/1747
        C(10)23 Goodeth Burdick b. 4/17/1751   m   Elisha Covey
        C(10)24 Tacy Burdick b. 10/12/1754
        C(10)25 Milety Burdick b. 2/11/1758   m.   Zaccheus Maxson
        C(10)26 Adam Burdick b. 12/28/1759 m.(1)4/17/1773 Hannah Burdick
                              m (2)   Lodema Lee
        C(10)27 Shephard Burdick b. 10/18/1766   m.   Lucinda_____
    C(10)3 John Burdick b. 5/19/1721 m. 12/1/1750   Elizabeth Babcock
        C(10)31 Maxson Burdick b. 1/22/1751   m   Chloe Lewis
        C(10)32 Thompson Burdick b. 9/1/1753   m.   Tabitha Wilcox
        C(10)33 Anne Burdick b.2/2/1775   m.   Simeon Bromley
        C(10)34 John Burdick, Jr. b.9/20/1756   m.   Elizabeth Beers
        C(10)35 Paul Burdick b..10/24/1759   m.   Mary Stanton
        C(10)36 Abigail Burdick b.11/22/1761   m.   Amos Chapman
        C(10)37 Sarah Burdick b.9/7/1763 m.   Reuben Peckham Maine
        C(10)38 Frances Burdick .b 3/29/1765   m.   Lymna Maine
        C(10)39 Joshua Burdick b.5/7/1768   m.   Katurah Hill

C(10)3(10) Elkanah Burdick b,.   m.   Martha Worden

C(10)3(11) Hannah Burdick   m.   Robert Brown

C(10)4 Ezekial Burdick b. 172___ m. 7/14/1750   Amey Downing

C(10)41 Amie Burdick b.6/29/1751   m.   Benjamin Lewis

C(10)42 Mary Burdick b.5/28/1753

C(10)43 Henry Burdick b.12/16/1755 m.   Judith Maxson

C(10)44 Huldah Burdick b.8/17/1758

C(10)45 Barbara Burdick b.10/17/1760

C(10)46 Rhoda Burdick b. 2/5/1763 d. 9/4/1764

C(10)47 Jared Burdick b.8/17/1767 d. 11/26/ 1786

C(10)48 Pardon Burdick b.12/25/1765 m.   Mary Lewis

C(10)49 Hannah Burdick b. 7/21/1772 m. Capt. Paul Babcock

[F77(11)]

C(11) Infant b. abt.1678 d. in infancy

D Rachael Hubbard b. 3/10/1642 m. 11/3/1658   Andrew Langworthy

D1 Samuel Langworthy b. abt. 1659 d. 1711 m.   Rachel _____

D11 Ann Langworthy d. 1773 m. 2/15/1716 Joseph Crandall, Jr [C43]
children listed under Joseph Crandall [see C43 }

D12 Samuel Langworthy d. 8/1/1763 m. 8/7/1736   Mary Crandall

D121 Mary Langworthy b. 5/1/1739

D122 Elizabeth Langworthy b. 5/31/1741

D123 Rachel Langworthy b. 6/8/1743 m. 10/5/1771   Timothy Larkin

D124 Samuel Langworthy b. 11/27/1745 d. 10/1/1818

D125 Tacy Langworthy b. 11/20/1747

D126 Joseph Langworthy b. 2/6/1749 d. 5/6/1824

D127 Hannah Langworthy b. 6/21/1752

D13 Rachel Langworthy abt.   d. 2/19/1745

D2 John Langworthy b. 1661 d. after 1692 bef. 1700 m. Elizabeth _____

D3 Andrew Langworthy   d. 1739

D4 Robert Langworthy b. abt. 1675 d. abt. 1720

D5 James Langworthy b. 1680 d. 1720

E. Samuel Hubbard b. 3/25/1644 d. soon

F. Bethia Hubbard b. 12/19/1646 m. 11/16/1664   Joseph Clarke[6]

F1 Judith Clarke b/10/12/1667 d. 7/1747 m. 1/19/1687 John Maxson, Jr

F11 Judith Maxson b. 9/23/1689

F12 Mary Maxson b. 10/26/1691 d. 3/16/1692

F13 Bethiah Maxson b. 7/31/1693 d. 1747m. abt. 1715 Joseph Maxson

[C81]

---

[6] Joseph Clarke was the nephew of Dr. John Clarke, the founder and first pastor of the First Baptist Church of Newport from which Seventh Day Baptists split. He was mentioned in Samuel Hubbard's list of those who came to the Sabbath in 1665 as "son Clarke."

F131 Bethia Maxson 10/19/1716 m. 1/5/1737   Thomas Davis
F132 Mary Maxson b. 8/28/1718 m. 3/__/1739 Joseph Stillman [C455]
F133 Judith Maxson b. 9/17/1720 d.1778 m.1/10/1740 James Davis
F134 Joseph Maxson b. 1/20/1723 m.   Elizabeth _____
F135 Zebulon Maxson b. 8/15/1725 d. 1787 m.   Experience Davis
F136 Simeon Maxson b. 8/25/1727 m 9/18/1754   Mary Babcock
F137 Content Maxson b. 12/31/1732 d. 1815 m.   George Potter
F138 Nathan Maxson b. 9/30/1736 m. 4/28/1764 Elizabeth Brown
F139 Ephraim Maxson b. 1743   d. 1799 m.   Elizabeth Davis

F14 Elizabeth Maxson b. ll/7/1695 d. 1751 m. 8/25/1715 Rev. John
                                                           Davis[7]
    F141 Elizabeth Davis   b. 4/17/1717 m.   Willaim Brand
    F142 William Thomas Davis b. 5/15/1719 m.12/8/1737 Tacy Crandall
    F143 Martha Davis b. 8/14/1721 d. 1756   m. Nathan Rogers [C254]
    F144 Rev. John Davis, Jr. b. 9/18/1723   m (1) Bethia Rogers [F13]
                    (2)   Mary (Saunders) Stillman
    F145 Rev. Joseph Davis b. 9/24/1726   m. (1)   Comfort Langworthy
                    (2)   Dorcas (Clark ?)
    F146 Ann Davis   b. 1/23/1728
    F147 Judith Davis b. 4/7/1731 m.   Thomas Babcock
    F148 Experience Davis
    F149 Mary Davis b. 12/5/1737 m. 1/3/1759   Elisha Stillman
F15 Hannah Maxson b. 6/13/1698 m.   Capt John Maxson [C82]
    F151 William Maxson b. 1/20/1718 m. 10/14/1743 Hannah Reynolds
    F152 Amos Maxson b. 3/16/1720 m.   Mary Witter
    F153 Joshua Maxson b. 2/1/1722 m 9/20/1742   Anna Slack
    F154 Isaiah Maxson b. 1/21/1724 m. 10/19/1749   Judith Reynolds
    F155 Goodeth Maxson b. 1/5/1726 m. 10/14/1743   Nathan Burdick
                                                       [C(10)2]
    F156 Tacy Maxson b. 12/15/1728 m. 1/22/1747   Jonathan Lewis

---

[7] Rev. John Davis was the son of Rev. William Davis who was born in
Wales in 1663 and came to America in 1684. He was a Quaker in Penn's
colony at Philadelphia. In 1696 he joined the Penepek Baptist Church and
became its pastor About 1698 he accepted the doctrine of the Sabbath and
helped organize a church in the Philadelphia area , the second Seventh Day
Baptist church in America. His descendents formed the nucleus of the
Shrewsbury New Jersey SDB Church, which, after the Revolutionary War
migrated to Salem, West Virginia. One of the brothers of John Davis,
Thomas Davis, married Bethia Maxson [F13], while several of his daughters
married into the Hubbard family: Martha married Rev. Nathan Rogers
[C254], Mary, married Elisha Stillman[C455]., Experience, married
Zebulon Maxson [F135] ,Judith married Thomas Babcock as his second
wife. A son, John Jr married Bethia Rogers [C257] while another son ,
William Thomas [F142] is listed as having married a Tacy Crandall.

96

F157 Judith Maxson b. 1/17/1731 m. 12/1/1749 John Matthew Greene
F158 Torey Maxson b. 1/22/1733 m. 1753   Martha Lanphere
F159 Silvanus Maxson b. 5/3/1735 m 12/21/1769   Lydia Lewis
F15(10) Hannah Maxson b. 12/3/1737 m. 12/21/1757 David Reynolds
F15(11) Mary Maxson b. 11/23/1739
F16 John Maxson b. 4/21/1701 d. 1786 m. 9/26/1724 Thankful Randall
F161 John Maxson b. 8/27/1725 m. 10/30/1746   Sarah Burdick
F162 Matthew Maxson b. 4/27/1727 d.1791 m.12/21/1749 Martha
                                                        Potter
F163 David Maxson b. 7/24/1729 d. 1786 m. 1748 Abigail Greenmen
F164 Joseph Maxson b. 3/23/1731 m. 9/11/1753 Keturah Randall
F165 Benjamin Maxson b. 2/21/1733 d. 1822 m. Eunice Reynolds
F166 Stephen Maxson b. 5/3/1735 d. 1794 m   Martha Stewart
F167 Thankful Maxson b. 7/16/1737 m.   Nathan Barber
F168 Daniel Maxson b. 9/23/1739 m (1) 3/31/1762   Borodell Ross
                        (2)   Anne_____
F169 Joel Maxson b. 5/28/1742 d. 1762
F16(10) Elinor Maxson b. 1/24/1749 m. 10/31/1771 Capt. WIlliam
                                                        Bliven
F17 Dorothy Maxson b. 10/20/1703 m. 7/24/1724 Thomas Burdick [C73]
        See C73 for children
F18 Susan Maxson b. 10/19/1706 m.   Zacheus Reynolds
F19 Joseph Maxson b. 12/__/1709 d.1710
F1(10) Avis Maxson b. 12/27/1712 m. 11/5/1731 Samuel Burdick [C16]
F2 Joseph Clarke b. 4/4/1670 d. 6/5/1719 m. (1) 1/5/1692 Dorothy Maxson
                        m (2)   Anna Babcock
F21 Freegift Clarke b. 7/4/1694 m.   John Saunders
F22 Dorothy Clarke b. 5/28/1696
F23 Experience Clarke b. 7/6/1699
F24 Joseph Clarke b d. 1783 m. 4/25/1728   Deborah Crandall
   F241Joseph Clarke b 3/5/1728 m. 12/26/1746   Hannah Perry
   F242 Anne Clarke b 10/23/1730   Samuel Perry Jr.
   F243 Joshua Clarke b 5/13/1733 m. 4/23/1760   Dorcas Smith
   F244 Samuel Clarke b 12/1/1737 m.9/16/1761 Susannah Stanton
   F245 John Clarke b 7/8/1740 d. 2/22/1836 m 1759. Sarah Gardiner
   F246 Oliver Clarke b. 11/21/1743 m. 12/16/1761   Mary Wells
   F247 Sarah Clarke b. 6/15/1745 m. 9/17/1761   Thomas Wells
   F248 James Clarke b.7/9/1748 m.
   F249 Christopher Clarke b.4/7/1751 m.
   F24(10) Amy   m.   _____Sheffield
F25 Elisha Clarke b. ll/17/1718 (from 2nd wife) m. 2/15/1743 Mary
                                                        Potter
   F251 Mary Clarke b. 1/12/1744
   F252 Anna Clarke b.10/7/1747 m. 1/6/1768   Joshua Pendleton
   F253 Elisha Clarke b.1/28/1750
   F254 Thomas Clarke b. 2/29/1752
   F255 George Clarke b. 1755 d. 9/22/1831 m. 1/29/1778 Keturah
                                                        Maxson

97

F256 Martha Clarke b.2/17/1757 m. 3/14/1782   Edward Saunders
F257 Joshua Clarke b.6/20/1759 2/16/1786   Wealthy Stillman
F258 Luke Clarke b. 10/10/1761
F259 John Clarke b.   m. 11/29/1804   Mercy Lanphere
F25(10) Lewis Clarke
F25(11) Hannah Clarke b. 1767 d.1848 m.10/21/1790 Arnold
                            Saunders
F3 Samuel Clarke b. 9/29/1672 d. 1769 m. (1) 1/19/1698   Anne Champlin
                (2) 5/26/1720   Susanna Champlin
F31 Samuel Clarke 1/19/1699   d. young
F32 Mary Clarke b. 11/27/1701
F33 Bethiah Clarke 7/18/1703
F34 Joseph Clarke 8/29/ 1705 d. 1783 m. 11/15/1727   Sarah Reynolds
F341 Amie Clarke b.8/23/1737 m. 3/3/1755 Jonathan Babcock
F342 Thankful Clarke b.2/23/1739 m. 3/9/1788 (2nd wife) Eld. John
                             Burdick [C161]
F343 Sanford Clarke b.10/7/1740 d. 1752
F344 Simeon Clarke b.8/28/1742 m. 10/22/1766 Hannah Champlin
F345 Gideon Clarke b.11/21/1744 d. 8/27/1752
F346 Bethiah Clarke b. 10/19/1746 d. 8/18/1752
F347 Esbon Clarke b.8/20 1748 d. 8/28/175
F348 Peleg Clarke b.7/20/1750 d. 8/22/1752
F349 Ann Clarke b. 7/30/1752
F35 Ann Clarke b. 9/3/1707
F4 John Clarke b. 8/25/1675 m. 11/1/1705   Mary Beebe
F41 John Clarke b. 9/4/1706
F42 Samuel Clarke b. 1/15/1707
F43 Mary Clarke b. 11/15/1709
F44 Ebenezer Clarke b. 7/1/1711 m. 9/12/1735   Ann Cooley
F45 Benjamin Clarke b. 6/21/1713 m. 11/3/1734   Grizzel Sherman
F451 Mary Clarke b. 9/17/1735
F452 Sherman Clarke b. 1737 m. 1/22/1756   Catherine Truell
F453 Peleg Clarke b. 5/26/1738
F454 Elizabeth Clarke b. 5/31/1739
F46 Elizabeth Clarke b. 6/19/1715
F47 Bathsheba Clarke b. 10/26/1717 m. (1)   John Mackee
F471 Bathsheba Mackee (Magee)
           m. (2)   Joseph Hiscox [F57]
F472 Clarke Hiscox b. 10/14/1760
F5 Bethiah Clarke b. 4/11/1678 d. 1756 m. 10/31/1703 Rev. Thomas Hiscox [8]
F51 William Hiscox b. 5/31/1705 m. (1) 1727 Susannah Burdick [C99]
F511 William Hiscox m. (2) 12/22/1742 Content (Maxson) Babcock
                             [C242]

---

[8] Thomas Hiscox was the son of Rev. William Hiscox a charter member
and first pastor of the Newport Seventh Day Baptist. He was the fourth
pastor of the First Hopkinton Church.

F512 David Hiscox b. 1743
F513 Susannah Hiscox b. 1745
F514 Content Hiscox b. 1747
F515 Lucy Hiscox b. 1749
F52 Ephraim Hiscox b. 6/2/1707   m. 1733   Abigail Saunders
   F521 Ephraim
F53 Edith Hiscox b. 9/6/1709 m. 5/2/1736 Joseph Crandall [C431]
F54 Bethiah Hiscox b. 1711 m.   Elder John Davis
F55 Mary Hiscox b. 7/12/1713 unmar.
F56 Thomas Hiscox b. 5/17/1715 m. 1754   Elizabeth Saunders
F57 Joseph Hiscox b. 4/22/1717 m. (1)   Sarah Green
                (2) 1754   Bathsheba Mackee [F471]
F58 Hannah Hiscox b. 1/22/1719 m. 1737   Jonathan Rogers [C252]
F6 Mary Clarke b. 12/27/1680 d. abt. 1760 m. 1/18/1699 William Champlin
  F61 William Champlin b. 5/31/1702
  F62 Jeffrey Champlin b. 3/6/1704
  F63 Joseph Champlin m. 1730   Deborah Burdick   [C74]
  F64 Samuel Champlin
  F65 Joshua Champlin
  F66 James Champlin
  F67 Susanna Champlin
F7 Susanna Clarke b. 8/31/1683 m. 1/___/1705   Oliver Babcock
  F71 Susanna Babcock b. 9/20/1705 m.   James Beebe
  F72 Thomas Babcock b. 3/7/1710 m (1)   Mary Davidson
    F721 Mary Babcock   m.   Simeon Maxson
    F722 Simeon Babcock   (2) m.   Judith Davis
    F723 Experience Babcock m.   John Davinson
    F724 Elizabeth Babcock m.   Henry LcLafferty
    F725 Thomas Babcock b. 2/12/1759   m.   Martha Davis
    F726 Amey unmarried
  F73 Mary Babcock b. 2/8/1713 m. abt. 1732   Henry Cobb
  F74 Nathan Babcock b. 10/12/1715
  F75 Simon Babcock b. 9/27/1717 m.   Sarah Gardner
    F751 Eunice Babcock b. 10/3/1744
    F752 Jeremiah Babcock b. 5/16/1746 m.   Susannah Rogers
    F753 Thomas Babcock b. 7/21/1748
    F754 Lucy Babcock b. 1/11/1750
    F755 Dorcas Babcock b. 12/1/1753
    F756 Jason Babcock b. 7/9/1756 d. 1/19/1842 m .   Mary _____
    F757 Lydia Babcock b. 6/20/1759
    F758 Hannah Babcock b. 4/28/1762
    F759 Lucas Babcock b. 4/24/1765
    F75(10) Jonathan Babcock b. 4/18/1768 m.   Priscilla Wheeler
  F76 John Babcock b. 5/12/1720
  F77 Oliver Babcock b. 9/16/1722 m.   Patience Pendleton
    F771 Oliver Babcock b. 6/28/1746 m.   Tacy Maxson
    F772 Peleg Babcock b. 10/4/1748   Lucy Maxson
    F773 Susann Babcock b. 6/25/1750   Mr. Fen

F774 Deborah Babcock b. 4/11/1752 m 2/26/1777 Nathaniel Stillman
F775 Lucy Babcock b.1754 m.   Benjamin Baker
F776 Sarah Babcock b. 4/27/1756 m.   Philemon Steadman
F777 Mary Babcock b. 6/11/1758 m.   Benjamin Baker
F778 Ruth Babcock b. 4/20/1760 m.   James Kenyon
F779 Clarke Babcock b. 6/10/1762 m.   ____Baker
F77(10) Ruhannah b. 5/16/1764 m.   Edward Denison
F77(11) Capt. Paul Babcock b. 5/18/1766 m.1/10/1788 Hannah
                                         Burdick [C(10)49]
F77(12) Ezra Babcock b. 9/16/1769 m.   Saberah Stillman
F77(13) Capt. Luke Babcock 8/6/1772 m.   Betsy Main
F78 Joseph Babcock b. 10/18/1726 m. 9/6/1757   Anna Harris
F781 Annie Babcock b.1/26/1758 unmar.
F782 Polly (Mary) Babcock b. 11/17/1760 m.   David Denison
F783 Harris Babcock b. 3/15/1763 m.   Sally Newell
F784 Lieut Joseph Babcock b. 7/29/1765 m.   Jane Wallace
F785 Fannie Babcock b. 12/7/1767 unmar.
F786 Darius Babcock b. 6/17/1770 m.   Louisa Beebe
F787 __allah Babcock b. 9/5/1774
F8 Thomas Clarke b. 3/17/1686 d. 1767 m. 1710   Elizabeth Babcock
F81 Sarah Clarke b.5/11/1712 m. 11/26/1730 Edward Burdick
F82 Thomas Clarke b. 3/4/1715 m. 5/27/1740   Thankful Violet
F821 Mary Clarke b. 4/15/1741 m 1/21/1761 Capt. Peleg Saunders
F822 Thomas Clarke b. 4/23/1743
F823 Abigail Clarke b. 7/12/1745 m. 1806   Ira Burch
F824 Nathan Clarke
F83 Rev. Joshua Clarke b. 4/26/1717 d. 1808 m. bt 1738 Hannah Cotrell
F831 Phineas Clarke b. 2/23/1740 m. 11/23/1763   Mary Babcock
F832 Joshua Clarke b. 817/1741 d. 1764
F833 Ethan Clarke b. 3/7/1745 m. 2/4/1776   Anna Ward
F834 Hannah Clarke b. 5/4/1747 m. 11/14/1779   John Dodge
F835 Thomas Clarke b. 6/10/1749 d. 5/28/1832 m.6/10/1770 Olive
                                           Marsh
F836 Elizabeth Clarke b. ll/14/1751 d.12/25/1831 m. 5/18/1770 Col.
                                         Jesse Maxson
F837 Arnold Clarke b. 3/17/1754 m.   Lucy Champlin
F838 Rev. Henry Clarke b. 12/2/1756 m. (1) 12/5/1776   Catherine
                                         Pendleton
               (2) 6/26/1825 Lydia Burdick
F839 Willet Clarke b. 10/20/1759 m. 4/1779   Sarah Pendleton
F83(10) Nathan Clarke b. 2/7/1762 d. 5/11/1776
F83(11) Job Bennet Clarke b. 5/13/1765 d. 1860 m. 1/1/1788 Mrs.
                                         Mary Wells
F84 James Clarke b. 3/3/1720 d. young
F85 Joseph Clarke b. 9/14/1728 d. 1795 m. 6/11/1752 Deborah
                                         Pendleton
F851 Sarah Clarke b. 6/24/1753 m. 3/20/1771   Silas Maxson
F852 Samuel Clarke b. 12/11/1754 m. 1776   Cloe Maxson

F853 Nathan Clarke b. 3/9/1756 m.   Sarah Maxson
F854 Nancy Clarke b. 5/24/1758 d. 1840 m.   Clarke Maxson
F855 Asa Clarke b. 5/25/1760 d. 1830 .m.   daughter of John Maxson
F856 Simeon Clarke b. 2/13/1762 d. 1850 m. (1)   Eunice Brown
                m. (2)   Betsey Burdick
   F857 Adam Clarke b. 2/11/1764 d. 1836 m.   Olive Burdick
   F858 Fanny Clarke b. 3/4/1766 d. 1850 m.   Robert Burdick
   F859 Jared Clarke b. 3/4/1768 d. 1800   unmar.
   F85(10) Abel Clarke b. 2/22/1770 m. (1)   Eunice Lanphere
               m. (2)   Mary Lanphere
   F85(11) Mary Clarke b.10/9/1772 d.1851 m.12/1/1791 Joshua Burdick
   F85(12) Ethan Clarke b. 12/17/1773 d. 1859 m.   Phebe Clarke
   F85(13) Joseph Clarke b. 9/20/1776 m. 2/1/1800   Hannah Clarke
   F85(14) Deborah Clarke b. 9/27/1778 d. 1826 m.   Asa Stillman
   F85(15) Benjamin Clarke b. 6/4/1781 m. 3/9/1803   Mary Stillman

F9 William Clarke b. 4/21/1688 m. 9/9/1709   Joan Bliven
  F91 Judith Clarke b. 7/7/1710 m. abt. 1729   Jonathan Burdick [C93]
   F911 Jonathan Burdick b. 4/1/1730 m.   Ruth Millard
   F912 Joseph Burdick b.11/10/1733 m.   Content Peckham
   F913 Oliver Burdick b 3/27/1735 m.   Lydia Elderton
   F914 Ruth Burdick b 12/10/1737 m.   Joseph Sheldon
   F915 Judith Burdick b 5/21/1740 m.   Joseph Johnson, Jr
   F916 Wealthy Burdick b 6/18/1743 m.   Jonathan Nash
   F917 Ephraim Burdick b 5/1/1746 m.   Anna Peckham
   F918 Benjamin Burdick b 8/27/1748 m.   Martha Huling
   F919 Asa Burdick b 8/6/1751   Isabel Davis
   F91(10) Hannah Burdick b. 10/29/1755   Clarke Crandall
  F92 Susannah Clarke b. 2/8/1711 m. 12/31/1730 Robert Burdick [C91]
  F93 Lucy (possibly) Tacy Clarke b. 2/21/1713
  F94 William Clarke 12/25/1715 d. 1759 m. 11/13/1749 Jemima Vincent
   F941 William Clarke b 1750 d. 1822 m.   Eunice____
   F942 Nicholas Clarke b 3/21/1752 m. 1/20/1779   Barbara Wells

G Samuel Hubbard b. 11/30/1649   d. 1/20/1670

Principal Sources for Hubbard Family Tree

Call numbers are from the
Seventh Day Baptist Historical Society Library and Archives

Church and Denominational Records

Newport Seventh Day Baptist Church Records 1692-1846 & First Hopkinton Seventh Day Baptist Church 1708-1714. Handscript copy by William J.Stillman 1850. (CRR 19x.78 Vault CRR)

Seventh Day Baptist Memorial 1852-1854 published quarterly by the Seventh Day Baptist Publishing Society (BX6390 S4 M44)

Seventh Day Baptists in Europe and America pub. American Sabbath Tract Society, Plainfield, NJ 1910 (BX 6393 A5 1910)

Samuel Hubbard's Journal 1633-1686, from typescript copy made by Roy Huling from Isaac Backus copy. (MS 194x. 6 A file)

A Choosing People: The History of Seventh Day Baptists by Don A. Sanford published by Broadman Press, Nashville TN Broadman Press 1992 copyright Seventh Day Baptist Historical Society, PO Box 1678 Janesville WI (BX6393 S26 1992)

Published Genealogies

BABCOCK: *Babcock Genealogy,* Stephen Babcock compiler, pub Easton & Main 1903 (CS71 B118)

BURDICK: *The Descendants of Robert Burdick of Rhode Island* by Nellie Willard Johnson printed by the Syracuse Typesetting Co., Syracuse NY 1937. (CS71 B949)

CLARKE: *The Clarke Families of Rhode Island* by George Austin Clarke Jr. printed by Press of the Evening Post Job Printing House 1954 (C71 M464)

ROGERS : *James Rogers of New London, Connecticut and His Descendants,* by James Swift Rogers, published by the Compiler Boston 1902 (C71 R73)

STILLMAN: *The Stillman Family - Descendants of Mr. George Stillman of Wethersfield, CT and Dr. George Stillman of Westerly RI* compiled by Francis D. Stillman Jr. 1989 (C71 S857)

NEWPORT TRILOGY INDEX

NASH, 101
NEWBURY, 90
NEWELL, 100
NICHOLS, 88
OCKFORD, 15
ODLIN, 74
OLNEY, 21
PACKHAM, 81
PAINTER, 73
PARKER, 82
PARTELO, 92
PEARCE, 81, 83-84.
PECKHAM, 73-74, 79, 84,
    89-90, 94, 101.
PENDELTON, 81, 93, 97, 99-100.
PERRY, 97
PETERSON, 52.
PHILLIPS, 18, 20, 61, 76-77,
    80, 90-91.
PICKENS, 82
PIERCE, 79, 89.
POTTER, 90, 96-97.
POTVIN, 16
POWERS, 89
PURSER, 14
QUEEN MARY, 90
RANDALL, 76, 93, 97.
RAY, 46
READ, 77
REED, 75, 79.
REYNOLDS, 92 , 94, 96-98
RHODES, 74, 88, 91.
RICHMAN, 88
RICHMOND, 92
RIDER, 79
RITTER, 78

ROADS, 76-77.
ROBINSON, 18, 88.
RODMAN, 81
ROELKER, 48
ROGERS, 4, 18, 20, 43, 56,
    74-78, 80, 85-86, 88-90,
    92, 96, 99, 102.
ROME, 53
ROSS, 97
RUSSELL, 79
RYON, 90
SABEAR, 74
SABIN, 75, 78, 80.
SALISBURY, 88
SALMON, 25-27.
SANFORD, 15, 51, 102
SATTERLEE, 94
SAUNDERS, 20, 43, 76-77,
    80-84, 87-88, 91-93, 96-100.
SAWYER, 89
SCISCO, 79
SCOFIELD, 79, 84.
SEAMAN, 79
SEARS, 83-84.
SHAIRMAN, 80
SHEFFIELD, 97
SHELDON, 101
SHELLY, 92
SHERMAN, 98
SHREVE, 80-81.
SISSON, 86, 88, 92.
SLACK, 92, 96.
SMITH, 17, 44, 74, 80-81,
    88-89, 93, 97
.SOLOMON, 74
SOUTHWICK, 34, 38-39, 59, 80.

STACY, 83
STANBOURCH, 79
STANTON, 94, 97.
STEADMAN, 100
STEED, 53
STENNETT, 15, 29-30, 54.
STEWART, 87, 94, 97.
STILES, 18, 34.
STILLMAN, 20, 31, 53, 56, 58,
    69, 76, 84-85, 90, 92, 96.
    98, 100-102.
STONE, 78
STOWE, 76
STUART, 53
SWEET, 90-91.
TANNER, 34-35, 47-51, 70-71,
    79, 81, 83, 92, 94.
TAYLOR, 86
TEFT, 92
TELFORD, 79
THOMAS, 78-79
THOMPSON, 89, 92.
THORNDON, 73
THORNGATE, 33
THORNTON, 20, 76.
THURSTON, 82-84.
TIFT, 77
TILLAM, 54
TILLEY, 38-39.
TORREY, 19, 27, 29, 74.
TRASK, 13
TREBY, 76, 78.
TRUELL, 98
TUCKERMAN, 78

TURNER, 53
UTTER, 94
VANDERBILT, 52
VARS, 93
VAUGHAN, 73
VERNON, 75, 78.
VICKERS, 78
VINCENT, 101
VIOLET, 100
WAIT, 82
WALLACE, 100
WARD, 7, 11, 15, 31, 34,
    44-47, 52, 58-69, 63, 69,
    71, 75-81,100.
WASHINGTON, 53
WATERHOUSE, 52
WAY, 84
WEEDEN, 32-33, 53, 73-74,
    76, 78, 81-82, 86.
WEEKS, 47, 78.
WELLS, 20, 91-93, 97, 100-101.
WEST, 73, 75-78, 80.
WHEELER, 99
WHITE, 79
WHITFORD, 93
WIGHTMAN, 73
WILCOX, 81-82, 84, 88, 93-94.
WILD, 74
WILKINS, 74
WILLIAMS, 8, 43-44, 46, 52, 73.
WITTER, 96
WORDEN, 95
WYLD, 25-27,
YORK, 88, 93.

Addendum to page 91

C4 Deborah Burdick m. Joseph Crandall
  C41 John Crandall m. (1) Mary_____
      C411 John Crandall
      C412 Deborah Crandall
      C413 Mary Crandall
      C414 Tacy Crandall m.
                    *Wm. Thomas Davis [F142]
      C415 Elizabeth Crandall

                        m. (2) Hannah _____
      C416 Levi Crandall
      C417 Abijah Crandall
      C418 Elijah Crandall
      C419 Martha Crandall
      C41(10) Hannah Crandall

                        m. (3) Elizabeth Lewis
      C41(11) David Crandall
      C41(12) Stephen Crandall

* Thus the children of William Thomas Davis,
also listed as Thomas William Davis are descended
from the Crandalls and the Burdicks
through Tacy Crandall , John Crandall, Deborah
Burdick, Ruth Burdick and Samuel and Tacy Hubbard